TIME TO CHANGE

GRAZING • GENETICS • MANAGEMENT

Leave the High Input

Low Net Profit System

Join the High Net Profit

Low Input System

By

CHIP HINES

TIME TO CHANGE

GRAZING • GENETICS • MANAGEMENT

ISBN 10: 1469937522

ISBN 13: 978-1469937526

CreateSpace, North Charleston, South Carolina

To my late wife, Judy, for all the good times together

TABLE OF CONTENTS

ACKNOWLEDGEMENTS

The idea of writing this book had been floating around in my head for several years before I decided to get to work. As always in an endeavor like this there are several people that help bring it about, even if they don't realize they did. The 'Bull Session' group that you will read about later, was the beginning of many hours of discussion that gave me the desire to express myself in a meaningful way. The group helped me to fully develop and expand my thinking on many things that I had observed and practiced through the years. Along with my thoughts I include all that I learned from the other members. The knowledge of many trumps one.

I owe more than I can ever repay to these original Bull Session members. Don Palmer, John Palmer, Kit and Deanna Pharo, Barbara Jolly, R.J. Jolly, Mike Merritt, Gordon Hatfield, Gary Rhoades, Bobby Rhoades, Earl Helm, Leroy Mosher and Cliff Roberts.

I also owe thanks to those who furnished information for clarifying certain pieces and those who allowed me to reuse parts of articles I had written about them in the newsletter my daughter, Mildy, and I published several years ago. You will find their names scattered throughout the book.

My daughters, Mildy and Dru, gave ol dad much needed help and support when needed, and that was often.

INTRODUCTION
Why this book?

The livestock industry in this country has been going down the wrong path for many years. Our net profit, which pays our living expenses and affords a certain life style, has been on a downward spiral for years. This will continue until major changes are made to individual operations. Also the degradation of our soil has to be recognized as a problem that can no longer be ignored.

Without a healthy environment, all that we aspire to will be difficult or non-attainable. All terrestrial life on this planet is dependent on sunshine, water, and soil. Each has its importance, but soil is the medium, which makes all else possible. Our soils have not been ignored, but their proper care is not really understood by vast numbers of livestock operators.

I want to stir imaginations, to change ways of thinking, to open minds, to shrink comfort zones, to encourage looking at what others have done, to make others realize change is possible by rearranging thought. I look at myself as a 'cheerleader', to induce people into full use of their intelligence. Most people who have done this find it exhilarating and don't look back once they have stepped over the edge.

For the last 40 years we have been in an era of increasing inputs, higher performance, and artificial environments. This has raised gross profits, but also has put a serious drag on net profit. Management techniques, grazing strategies, and genetics can cut reliance on these costly inputs that are constantly on the rise. Any input not purchased is one step closer to a profit.

My ranching experience has been in the semi-arid, shortgrass country of Eastern Colorado, but the basics are the same in all regions of the country. The basics include overall management, grazing management and genetics. Once these are understood, the thinking starts. Every ranch, in every area, in every environment, must then make the needed adjustments to fit their operations.

This is a 'why not' instead of a 'how to' book. Before someone can move to the 'how to' stage they must be convinced of the value of a new process. When the level of understanding reaches a place that logic can take over and direct thinking in the new direction, the 'how to' stage is in place.

Without a first step, nothing is ever accomplished. If this book will encourage just a few people to take that first step I will feel I have accomplished my goal.

A NEW DIRECTION

TIME TO CHANGE

As every industry matures it gradually changes in keeping with the times. Sometimes in the right direction. Sometimes not. The American cattle industry is guilty of shifting to a high input, technical model of ranching that ignores the natural world foundation that our industry is built on. This slide started quite gradually, but picked up speed as change was piled upon change. As with any incremental adjustment, it was not until those that walk a little slantwise to the crowd realized we were building an artificial environment that was fast becoming non-sustainable.

Where did we go wrong? Partly it is the American system. Bigger, better, faster. Out with the old. In with the new. Mankind ever marching forward, with new 'gee whiz' technology. Advanced technology is quite successful in the world of iron, electronics, concrete, manufacturing, which are systems manipulating inorganic materials.

We have a unique position in that our livelihood depends on working with living matter that does not bend to the will of mans' desires. Every living thing, whether plant or nimal, has its own course, laid down in genetics developed over thousands of years of natural selection. The natural world cannot be bulldozed into doing what we want.

Our main effort should be to simplify livestock operations with nature as the guide. The first thing we must do is carefully study nature, especially the symbiosis between plants and animals to bring back the original fertility of our soils. Without a deep understanding of these systems, and how they work, we are stumbling in the dark.

One of Einstein's quotes is very apt in working our way out of the non-sustainable situation we have fallen into.

"The significant problems we face today cannot be solved at the same level of thinking with which we created them."

This is the hard part. To completely rearrange our thinking and let go of what we were sure was the right way and learn a different system. The 'high input' thinking has to be kicked out to make way for a process of logical decision-making that concentrates on a low input, net profit method of management with the natural world as the basis of our operations. Everything under our management has to be observed, evaluated and made to work together in a complimentary system.

A good way to change thinking is to join with others interested in the same direction. Ignore those that are negative, the 'ain't no way it will work here' people, and stay away from the places they congregate.

Support groups are positive in their thinking, willing to evaluate new thought, and harbor a deep sense of logic. They will strengthen resolve to make the needed changes for survival in a world where the rules are changing to a way of thinking that requires a lot of contemplating to grasp the basics. This newfound direction may lead to a life long passion after the tipping point is reached.

The cow-calf and yearling portions of our industry have veered off course drastically in the last 50 years. This has allowed our operations to degrade into a high input system that supports everyone, but us. We cannot stay on this track. Every penny of profit needs to be for our benefit. The American cattlemen cannot be the cash cow for everyone who thinks that what they are selling will make us huge profits. Inputs are sucking off the profits and leaving us with a small amount of leftovers.

Today's world is not the slow, stable place of business that your dad and/or granddad dealt with. We can see more changes in one week than occurred in months or years back in the fifties. It is easier to predict droughts than figure out what politicians and world leaders will stir up next. The only way to survive drought, low prices, blizzards, politics and other maladies is to keep expenses at a bedrock low, just like our ancestors.

Low input ranching uses management instead of money to solve problems. What could be more cost effective? Low input is a state of mind. This will take some training, but as one learns to use imagination and knowledge to make decisions, it opens the mind to other possibilities. This knowledge feeds on itself and will lead you to higher levels of reasoning.

If there is very little outgo that means the income you bring in is yours and does not have to be shared with others. Remember, the important thing is not how much you bring in, but how much you keep. Concentrate on this. Those selling inputs, whether pharmaceuticals, machinery or chemicals, etc, aren't concerned with how much money you make as long as you stay in business (barely) and continue to support them.

We allowed ourselves to be led into a system geared to inputs and flawed management that did not have a focus on net profit. Everything we read led us to believe a high level of production would lead to a more profitable operation. Do more. Spend more. Baby the cow more. Buy more machinery. Buy more chemicals. Buy more antibiotics. More labor. More everything. It didn't work, but those folks are still out there with their hand extended.

Look at last year's expenses. And the year before. And the year before that. Higher every year aren't they? Are these expenses rising at a percentage rate faster than income? No need to say anything, as I know the answer. Do you think this eternal increase will ever slow down? Have you ever bought a pickup, piece of machinery, chemical or pharmaceutical that cost less than the year before? Doubtful.

The long-term survival of ranchers will be tied to net profit. If you can change your thought processes to adapt to this style of thinking, it will be possible for your ranch to still show a net profit when times are tough and continue on into the future.

There is no one perfect way to manage a ranch because of a myriad of variables and environments to take into account. Several basic facts of management fit almost everywhere and should be the backbone of your operation. The basics are the hard part as this is where the brain has to let go of the old way of doing things and accept something foreign. It is a downhill run if you can get around that roadblock. The mind will accept incremental moves to refine management technique, which is what this is all about.

At this time something else needs to be considered. As we concentrate on something considered a problem it possibly takes on an importance not deserved. A New Zealand farmers' approach should be used. "When you have a problem, first look for a no cost answer. If one can't be found, then look for a low cost answer. If that fails, stop and look over the problem. It is quite possible you don't have a problem."

This is very true. Often a problem is only perceived. We tend to think everything must be just so so and don't realize that we may be worrying about some fluff that is inconsequential and could be ignored. The world will not come to an end if we let some things slide. As you sharpen management, these things will be much easier to spot (and ignore).

Greg Matney of Lusk, Wyoming found the following in a book published by the American Angus Assn. in the early 1960's. Why did we forget such an admonishment?

"A man with a cow herd is never certain how much his calves will be worth when they reach market age-so he must keep all costs at a minimum to help insure a profit.

A. J. Schuler, Jr Fairview Angus Farm

"The farther back you can look, the farther forward you can see."

Winston Churchill

IF ONE CAN, THEY ALL SHOULD

Every so often in our lives something comes along to confound what we thought was the only way. We just knew it had to be done this way, or else. I've been blindsided by several, but one of the first really got me to thinking about genetics and wondering where had we gone wrong?

In 1974 I bought some cows that had always been wintered on cornstalks or other crop aftermath. Wintering on grass was a different world for these cows. Along in the winter when I started caking, they had no idea what I was pouring on the ground. No concept that it was food. After several days of watching the other cows gobbling it up, all but one learned what it was.

That had me worried, since without the extra protein to help extract nutrients from the winter grass, she would probably winter poorly and most likely come up open in the fall (standard thought). I mentally marked her for culling. Was I ever surprised when she checked bred? And again the next year. And the year after that. And that wasn't all. Every year her calf was a little above average in weaning weight.

I began to wonder what the heck was going on here. Without eating several dollars worth of protein, she was still in the herd and productive! And then it hit me.

16

If one can, they all should!' Was this one cow a strange creature, or is this the way they all could be?

Surely, I mentioned this to a couple of friends, but it ended there. I hadn't yet reached the point of having enough courage in my convictions to act on them. Worse yet, even after I started making multiple changes in management, I never quite got to the point of feeding no protein. I got close, but not quite.

At the same time this was going on I was giving a lot of thought to other problems. I might as well say it now, as it can't be hidden. I raised Herefords, as did my dad and granddad along with all the attending problems of the breed. My dad didn't think anything of having to milk out a few cows. "They're good cows", he would say. Well, yes they may milk well, but what about the labor and hassle of having to catch them and milk them down a little and get the calf started? There was also an occasional prolapse.

And of course a few bad eyes. Dad did start looking for bulls with pigment around the eyes in later years, and freely admitted that breeding for that pure white eye was a mistake. As I began putting together my operation, I decided I was going to make some changes away from what was figured the norm for Herefords.

I started culling rigorously for poor udders, prolapses and eyes. I wanted fault free cows to make calving less labor intensive and to cut down on culling for physical defects. I worked diligently on this for several years, making some progress, but not nearly enough. It was then that I realized the problems were coming down from the seedstock producers. They weren't culling for the things I deemed important. It was all about performance.

There is little reason to put up with genetic problems in your cows. The understanding and use of genetics can eliminate those defects by dedicated selection and culling. It is as simple as that. Selecting for what is needed and culling what is detrimental. In nature, the process usually ended in death or lack of production to bring about change. We need not go to this extreme. Sell the offenders and propagate the survivors.

Two goals need to be put in place. Removal of all genetic flaws and building a cowherd that can survive on what is grown on your ranch. This requires unmerciful culling and a level of dedication that cannot be stopped. If you falter just a bit, progress will go by the wayside.

Many commercial producers believe that all the problems of production are just the way it is supposed to be if you are in this business. That is absolutely wrong. These problems can be solved or at least relegated to a minor status. It takes imagination and hard work, but the payoff is more profit through using genetics and management instead of throwing money at the problem and applying huge amounts of labor for something that should occur naturally.

This will work, if you keep one thing in mind. "If one can, they all should.

THE NATURAL WORLD

In genetics and grazing man has tended to ignore, for the most part, how everything works in nature. Over many thousands of years the genetics of plants and animals determined growth and survival. A sort of symbiosis developed between the two. This covers many varieties of plants and animals, but in this instance we are concerned only with grasses, forbs and other plants eaten by domesticated livestock.

The plants depend on livestock to eat the top growth, which allows for new nutritious re-growth. The animals depend on this nutrition to sustain life. In return their urine and defecation return nutrients to the soil for the plants to use again. In the wild any animal that died passed back all that the body contained, thus giving a 100% or near 100% return to the soil. This natural fertilization and mineralization kept soil condition optimal and benefited the animals with excellent grazing.

In the western section of this country, deer, antelope, elk and buffalo are the animals usually associated with grazing forages before man introduced cattle, sheep, horses and goats. These wild grazing herds were on the move, grazing from one area to another. It would usually be some time before the herds returned to a certain area. In this fashion grasses and other plants were allowed to re-grow beforebeing bitten again. The plant remained healthy and productive with this rest period.

Then along came man. Not understanding how and why plants needed to be grazed in a certain fashion and not perceiving how survival genetics formed functional livestock he unknowingly began to devise his own systems that were counter productive to what was actually needed.

This led to lower production by plants and livestock that then needed help by man to survive. In this way we are fighting nature instead of working with her and tweaking what we could to make the natural system more productive.

To determine how to shape the future, the past must be studied for all naturally occurring processes. This will prevent throwing money (inputs) at problems instead of working within the natural system. Alan Savory said that we have to get to "the root cause of a problem to solve it." If not we are only treating symptoms and that is costly and never ending.

People have been trying to solve problems with inputs for a long time, but in the last 50 years it has gotten out of control. The input industry appears to have mind control over us. Producers tend to believe the propaganda that no one can make money without multiple, costly inputs.

Technology doesn't take into account that the natural world may bend a little but ultimately will fight back in some way. Another obstacle is that research usually only looks at a part of a problem and not the whole.

Since everything is inter-connected, all systems must be looked at together. Tinker with one thing and you throw something else out of kilter. When you try to adjust that portion something else is affected. All the parts have to be studied at the same time and any change must be in tune with the whole system. That can be very difficult, but must be done. Studying and understanding how a system works on it's own will make these changes much easier and less likely to disrupt the whole.

Actually, if we truly understand the natural system, we probably don't need to make very many changes. The efficiency is built in. Our only change should be to put aside mans disruptive tampering and allow nature to lead us. This mind change will be the hardest of all. For some it will be impossible. Especially when input supported, "freebie", magazines are assisting.

Man always thinks he can make things better and just cannot keep his hands off. The natural system is very simple. Study it, apply the known facts, and stand back.

WHO IS LEADING?

"If the people lead, the leaders will follow."

The sub-title above is absolutely correct. People on the land are in the forefront of remaking the cattle industry into a profitable and environmentally focused business. For the last 50 years most university cattle and grazing research, along with their teachings, have been out of touch with what was actually needed on the land. Their big push has been to ratchet up inputs and defy nature, with no recognition of net profit having a place in this design.

Whether plant or animal, all out performance and high production, was the centerpiece of most university research. Programs were focused on a very small part of a certain production system. This failure to look at all parts and tie everything together and the absolute incomprehension of the need to track NET profit led to systems adding tremendous costs without a redeeming return.

Through the years there were many unsung operators on the land that either resisted or just paid no attention to the goings on from above. The 'progressives' who said, "They just don't get it", ridiculed these stalwarts. These were pretty resolute characters to hang in there and ignore the pressure to fall in line.

Individuals in the livestock community are the leaders in devising workable and repeatable management strategies that are real world. They are not based on a tightly drawn research project that has a sharp focus on only one or two points. It is not possible for universities, using present methods, to come close to what is happening on ranches today. To keep up, universities will have to devise completely different research models.

While thinking about this I looked up the definition of empirical. I had only heard of the empirical method and didn't know what it entailed. My dictionary had several simple definitions. I then went to wikipedia and found it got more complicated, so I stayed with the dictionary. These two definitions are very close to what ranchers are practicing. 1. Depending altogether upon the observations of phenomena. 2. Depending on experience or observation alone, without due regard to science and theory.

Observation and experience are crucial in working out grazing and management plans. There may be science attached to these two, but it must fit within the variables of nature. Without this base it will lead to higher input costs and inefficient management.

It is my opinion that universities should do more monitoring of successful ranch operations instead of concentrating so much on their own research. There will always be gaps that dedicated research can fill, but the majority of learning should be on actual operations, in actual conditions, with a focus on better environmental conditions AND an improved NET profit.

The real leaders are those making daily observations and decisions that affect their livelihood. Every area of the country has these leaders and as they are identified and their practices emulated, progress will be sure and steady.

The rancher on the land, using good monitoring and evaluation, can make changes as needed, whether yearly, monthly, or day-by-day. This constant observation and re-planning keeps everything on track regardless of changing conditions. Mistakes will still be made, but they can be remedied as needed, before getting out of hand.

Many universities are gradually beginning to accept new grazing and management models and are improving their work in these fields, but still aren't able to accept anything very radical. This leaves the field wide open to allow those walking slantwise to be the true leaders in new thought. These are the ones to follow!

"My grandfather once told me that there are two kinds of people: Those who do the work and those who take the credit. He told me to be in the first group because there is less competition."
Indira Ganhdi Prime Minister of India 1966-77;1980-84

THINK LONG TERM

For quite some time the cattle industry has been stranded in a standard procedure type of management dependent on multiple profit lowering inputs. It is difficult to break away from something that has become second nature to succeeding generations of producers. It is the proverbial 'rut'which cannot be steered out of, even when new thought arrives. And new thought is here, based on the natural world that has been ignored for many years. Enlightened management of our present environment must be used instead of costly inputs.

The decision to take off on a new path can be uncomfortable, but where to start may be even worse. A number of changes need to taken into consideration and put into action to change the course of management. These can be separated into three seemingly unrelated groups, but ultimately are interconnected. In this way they are complimentary to each other and increase the degree of success.

The three management items are; overall management, grazing/soil management, and genetic management. Since all terrestrial life is dependent on soil life, this needs to be the main focus of your new direction.

Overall management and genetic management changes are easier to implement and can begin the process of getting

25

you on the road to profitability. Grazing management can be worked on at the same time, but takes longer to implement and gain the experience necessary to properly monitor, evaluate and re-plan to keep everything on track.

No one knows how long it will take to bring various soils back to something near the productivity level before mans' interference, but it must begin. We cannot continue to destroy soil fertility and at the same time expect an increase in profitability. If we do make strides in recovering lost fertility, it must not stop there. It should be looked at as an ongoing perpetual process that never ends.

"Long range planning does not deal with future decisions, but the future of present decisions."

Peter Drucker

I do not understand why politicians continually open their mouths and make stupid comments. Surely, they know better, but that said, I'm glad they do because that is the only way we know their actual thoughts and private leanings, which they don't want anyone to suspect.

Chip

THE BULL SESSION

If you are serious about making changes in your operation or are still in the incubating phase, get involved with others of a like mind. There is no better way to get the juices flowing and stimulate new thought or revamping the mind to accept something initially foreign.

While attending a ranch seminar and tour in 1990 with a friend, Don Palmer, he suggested we get some guys together and talk about these things. I agreed and that was our start. Don called several guys he thought would be interested while I did the same. I also called Kit Pharo and explained our idea and he contacted a few prospects. We didn't really know what we were going to do, or how, but that didn't slow us down.

I had already fenced my place and was one year into planned grazing management, so the first meeting was at our ranch on a Sunday afternoon. About a dozen guys showed up the first time. We toured my operation and began discussing what I had developed and where I was headed. Someone volunteered to be the next host and we were off and running. The first time around we met at a different ranch each meeting. After touring the place to better understand the workings, we concentrated on that operation during our discussion, with occasional digressions.

We usually met September through May. During the summer and at times in the winter we made trips to other

27

operations when we heard of someone doing something out of the ordinary. There would be from three
to as high as eight on these road trips, with a couple being overnighters. The ride to and from one of these trips was never boring. They were the setting for long, stimulating conversations. With the unique personalities involved in our group, what else could there be?

After getting the bull session underway, we began wondering if there were others opposing or rethinking a way of management that had gradually lost focus on profitability with a mindset of high production and creating artificial environments. Eventually we did find independent thinkers to link with. We met some great people and toured ranches off the beaten path of 'so called' progressive operations. Each one of these trips brought more knowledge into our discussions, opening up further management possibilities.

The meetings would generally start at 2:00 P.M and go to about 5:00. The host family, or as in some instances a single guy, would serve hamburgers or sloppy joes and the talk might continue a little longer. The meal was a low key and relaxing time. At one point we tried setting a main agenda, but usually we just freewheeled into a discussion that went from topic to topic, depending on the interest. Most of us had been on the high production bandwagon for a time, but knew it wasn't working and were looking for a new direction.

Our combined information and thoughts were synergistic. After a member stated an opinion or experience, others would add something. Each person fed on another, thus picking up energy to carry the discussion forward. It is nothing short of amazing what can be accomplished with several people working on a problem. Each person brought something new to the discussion. No two people have the very same thoughts. No two people look at a problem in the same way. No two people have the same experiences. No two people grew up in the same situation, and the list goes on.

This evolved into a powerful philosophy and direction that would have been difficult for any one person to formulate, as we had such a large base of knowledge and practical experience to work from. This combination of different thoughts coming from several directions, being hashed out and clarified by logic and common sense was nothing short of inspiring. We managed to put together a seemingly 'ordinary' group of people that were capable of 'extraordinary' reasoning.

Even to this day I'm not sure if we fully realize what we accomplished. I know it might not seem like much to some, but for me it was satisfying and fulfilling. And it relieved me of a great amount of stress, of fear of doing the wrong thing. Again.

We were spread out about 75 miles east to west and close to 110 miles north and south. Our operations ranged from deep sand to loam, from commercial to seedstock, from all grass, to grass and farm land, from 11 inch to 16 inch precipitation, from tallgrass to shortgrass. Most of us were friends or had at least heard of the others.

Possibly most important in our success was that none were regulars at the coffee shop. I'm not saying those who attend coffee shop whine sessions can't be involved in something like this, but they will have to let their memberships lapse. Coffee shops are negative. Our group was positive, and that is an absolutely necessary trait for any person pursuing continual management upgrading.

Other than our love of ranching, there was one other thing that helped make the bull session work. Humor. It was there all the time. Some of these guys couldn't help themselves. They opened their mouth and something funny came out. It has to be fun. Too much serious conversation can have a dampening effect. If something is very enjoyable it will bring everyone back. A group like this is successful only with good participation. It was this desire to take part, to discuss, evaluate and brainstorm that kept everyone coming back, meeting after meeting, year after year.

Over the years we invited some who only came a few times then dropped out. We jelled into a hard-core group of eight to ten that seldom missed a meeting. It was the most mind-stimulating project I have ever been associated with. We share a friendship that is very important, a bond that will be with us for the rest of our lives.

The mind stimulating part really came to the fore when one member gave up tickets to a Denver Bronco's-Kansas City Chiefs game to come to the meeting. His wife thought he had completely lost it. That impressed on all of us the extent we were involved.

I would like to encourage others to give this a try. It could be one of the most important steps you take, not only for the ideas and information, but also for the support of like-minded people. When someone brought up something new, they were forced to defend their position, but then they were supported in the endeavor. This is very important, as many good ideas are never acted on because the person feels alone out there on the fringe and is afraid to act for fear of failure and ridicule.

One thing I would stress to anyone interested in setting up a group is to set a meeting date and keep it, even if some can't make it. Trying to satisfy everyone each time is self-defeating. If people really want to make it they will think ahead in making appointments and setting work schedules. In the beginning we met on Sundays, but later moved to a weekday, as this was considered part of our everyday work and should be treated as such.

Several heads working together are more likely to foresee most problems and find solutions. It is very difficult for one person to do this. When working out a problem, one person is likely to concentrate on certain things and miss something else. A second person may see another aspect and a third person may see something else entirely different. In this way all angles will be investigated. It is easy for the brain to lock in on one thing and mire down. A group is much more likely to be all encompassing in their evaluation of a problem.

Even though I have mentioned guys a couple of times above we also invited women, other than the ranch hostess, to the meetings and a few did attend. Barbara Jolly and

Deanna Pharo attended on a fairly regular basis. Their input was as important as any other. Women tend to have a somewhat different perspective, which is very helpful when working on problems. Never overlook a woman's experience and views.

My youngest daughter Dru was in high school when the bull sessions were started and after sitting through two or three wrote the following about us. Leave it up to a kid for a different (honest) perspective.

THE BULL SESSION
Once a month they meet
to talk ranch talk

They discuss better ways
to raise cattle

They tell "horror" stories
of things gone wrong

They talk about parties
women and beef

They tell each other of an idea or two
they think would make things easier

They talk all afternoon about the
ifs ands and butt of some bull

> They attempt to figure out how many
> cattle can be sorted in an hour
>
> They brag about some cow or bull
> their wife or kids
>
> When they leave they need their boots
> because the bull is so deep
>
> Dru Hines

MY NEIGHBOR'S CRAZIER'N HELL!

Go see that guy! Go see that guy! The crazy guy is the one that sees things differently. He sees things clearly. He is a terrific observer. He has a gifted sense of logic. He can see solutions others can't. He walks slantwise to the crowd and doesn't care what the crowd thinks. And he is making a difference!

While the crowd is following down the same path they have traveled for years, this guy has veered off to the side and is mentally formulating new thought. This is out of the mainstream where he won't be swept away by 'normal' thinking and the negativity of people that try to hold everyone back, saying, "That won't work here."

These are the true thinkers. They are causing tidal waves that will carry others to an even higher level of thought. Associate with them. Learn from them. Try to understand how their thought processes work. Most people are much more capable than they realize. Once a threshold of ability to learn is reached there are no limits to what you may achieve. Challenge your brain! Spend more time thinking than doing! This thinking time is where solutions are derived. Without taking time to truly think you are just meandering and not challenging yourself.

Every community has one or more of these guys of varying degrees of intensity. Some may just be starting out on the new track, working things out as they go. As they get comfortable in their management, one step leads to another. This can lead to another idea, either adding to something already being done, or branching out to something else that captivates the imagination.

Others may be following the path granddad laid out many years ago when being conservative was the only way. Cattle had to survive with what the land could provide with management being the focus, because at the time very few purchased inputs were available or affordable. Some producers were rooted so strongly in that environment they kept to that path while others were adding inputs and following every new technology that came along.

These slantwise thinkers have some things in common that set them apart when it comes to management. They have a high level of curiosity, an exceptional ability to work through problems while keeping things simple, and use management and the natural world for the basis of their operation. They also are not satisfied with status quo. They believe there always can be improvements to any part of an operation. This stimulus drives them to even higher levels of problem solving.

Something else that tends to be universal among this group is the willingness to share their knowledge with others. When you hear of one of these guys, make contact, and if at all possible go look over the operation, study his methods and soak up his knowledge. It will be time well spent.

THE HALE'S DEMISE

A good friend, Ron Rehfeld, tells of a little incident he and his brother-in-law Bruce were involved in several years back. It all started when Bruce called him one morning and asked if he could help trailer some heifers home from a distant pasture? Of course Ron expected this to be something simple and un-eventual when he said, "Sure, he'd be glad to help." Boy was he wrong!

After the third or fourth load home they were heading back to the pasture with their empty trailers. Along the way, Bruce, who was in the lead, met a neighbor he wanted to talk to. He slammed on his brakes and waved at the guy, attempting to get his attention. Didn't work. He was 'movin on' concentrating on his driving and didn't notice Bruce trying to flag him down. This was just over the brow of a hill, and as Ron topped the hill, he met the neighbor spraying rocks and gravel. Ron said, "When the rocks started hitting my windshield I automatically ducked. When I looked up there wasn't any dust flying up behind Bruce's trailer! It was stopped! Uh, oh!"

Ron instantly stood on his brakes, (So hard his leg hurt the next day) and slid down the hill into, well, make that onto Bruce's trailer. It was an old Hale, one of the pipe and wood slat kind that put up little resistance to big cows and none to four wheel drive Chevy's. With pipes bending and wood shattering and flying around, Ron's pickup came to rest loaded on the Hale.

Yep, clear up over the trailer fenders. Ron bailed out and ran to see if Bruce was okay. Bruce was headed back to check on Ron, fearing he was hurt. They passed each other in the middle of the road and had to double back. You okay? Are you okay? After deciding they had survived with no injuries it was time to survey the damage. And damage there was. A lot! It was obvious, even to their untrained eyes, that the Hale would never haul cattle again.

And Ron's pickup wasn't in much better shape. The front axle no longer resided where it had when it left the factory.

It was set back into a new location, one not envisioned by Chevrolet engineers. His long wheelbase pickup had turned into a short wheelbase rig. It looked suspiciously like the clown jalopies that went bucking and rearing around the arena at a rodeo. The steering wheel even had a new shape. Ron had pushed on it so hard during the crash that each side was bent down. With his elbows locked, he didn't need a seat belt. Or an air bag. The front of Ron's pickup was sprouting various lengths of wood and pipe. Kinda' disfigured.

Did this put a halt to their days work? Nope. Just slowed them down a bit. In the best cowboy tradition they made do with what they had left. They got the Hale jerked out from under the Chevy and dragged it off into the ditch. They then unhooked Ron's pickup and pulled it into the ditch next to the matching trailer. They hooked the one good pickup to the remaining trailer and started out again. A little slower with one rig, but this time they could visit while driving. AND it was a whole lot safer with both of them in the same pickup!

Oh, yeah. First time they got close to a phone, they called the sheriff and told him, "You might want to take a look at a strange appearin' wreck in the ditch out here."

The Sheriff stood at the edge of the road looking down at the mangled iron in the ditch thinking, "There's some things they just don't teach in Sheriffin' school!" "Damn cowboys anyway!" "Why didn't they do this on the other side of the county line?"

REBUILDING SOIL

SETTING MY DIRECTION

In everyone's life there are circumstances that guide their thinking and direction in life's endeavors. Like most people my younger years were a formative time. The drought and dirt storm days of the 1950's left a lifelong impression on my thinking. Even though the failure of crops, lack of grass for grazing and terrible cattle prices were significant, it was the dirt storms and the following devastation that is forever embedded in my mind.

It is hard to describe a dirt storm to those who have never experienced one lasting a couple of days. When the lights were on all day long. The only work done outside was to do the chores. Schools were let out early to try to get kids home while there was some visibility. Or days when there was no school. Zero visibility along fields. Eyes continually full of dirt. Dirt drifting over roads like snow. Dust floating around in vehicles. Nothing airtight.

Airliners reporting dust in the air at 30,000 feet. Miles of fenceline buried in blow dirt that had to be pulled out and hung up on posts in the best way possible to keep cattle in, nowing it was temporary, because the wind would come again. Watching a dirt storm thousands of feet high rolling in, enveloping the land in darkness. An eerie awe-inspiring sight even when knowing the damage it would leave behind. Grass on the south side of fields covered with dirt for a hundred yards, much farther in some places. Straggles of grass with the roots exposed and the crown barely hanging on.

These memories were always in the back of my head in later years when I began managing my own operation. I have always had an affinity with grass that has led me to studying and improving the plant for my cattle. This has been a long journey, but very rewarding in the end.

When the rains came back, the ruinous effects of the dirt storms receded much quicker than I thought possible. This recovery exhibited the resilience of the land and its plants. It was hard to believe even as I watched it happen. But, even with this regenerative capacity, more needs to be done. We have only scratched the surface on rebuilding our soil to something resembling what was present at the end of the buffalo days.

In my early changes of grazing management, my thinking was concentrated on grasses. At the time I hadn't quite realized that I was actually building soil while improving my grass production. Soil is the backbone, the heart of terrestrial life. Proper grazing management is the process to feed the soil with the required nutrients to not only sustain, but also build more fertility.

I wonder what I could have done with this knowledge 45 years earlier. The past is gone, but the future is still ahead for a younger generation, and getting this message to them is one of the most important things I can do in life.

SOIL; THE ESSENTIAL MEDIUM

Soil is life. Every plant and animal on earth is dependent on soil for its sustenance. And yet we do not treat our soil with the importance it deserves. In many instances it is taken for granted and more attention is focused on something of lesser value.

It is common to fixate on what is easily observed. To ignore what we don't understand. To gloss over what is always there. And yet soil is the medium that makes all life possible. We tend to concentrate on moisture, sun and plants in our management, but without soil to sustain all the chemical reactions and microorganisms that derive fertility, there would be no life. This has to change. The study of soil and the application of proper processes have to be at the head of the list to get increased production from the land while improving the environment at the same time. These go hand in hand.

There has been continuing research on soil erosion and what fertilizers and chemicals to apply, but without a sufficient understanding of what is actually going on under the surface and how it can be enhanced. Again, we have to partner with nature instead of trying to bend it to our will.

There is a continual flow of information coming out about the actual inter workings of soil, water, sunlight and plants. The study and understanding of these procedures is the most important step we can take. We must take control of the process for making healthy soil, and place our greatest emphasis on this critical element.

The conservationist Aldo Leopold once said, "the study of plants and animals is important, but more important, is the relationship between plants and animals." We now know that this relationship has a direct bearing on the health of our soils. We need to concentrate our efforts to fully understand what is going on in our soil and what is required in grazing management to bring soil to its most fertile state.

Researchers are continually discovering more about the underground happenings, which is important, but this needs practical application on the land to reach its full potential. It will be the practitioners on the land, those with imagination that have no fear of experimentation, incorporating every facet of management, who will put it all together and make the process viable.

Organic matter is one of the main components of the process involved in producing a regenerative soil and has a direct relationship with grazing pressure. A healthy plant is one, which when bitten off by the grazing animal, is allowed to return to full height before being grazed again. At the same time roots are stimulated to grow much deeper into the soil, thus tapping into more nutrients and moisture. When the plant is again eaten, part of the root, along with energy in the leaf, furnish reserves for above ground growth. The depleted portion of the root dies and then becomes organic matter, which is the foundation for soil functions.

This continuous recycling of growth and harvest, carried out by wildlife for thousands of years, is necessary for soil health and rejuvenation. Continuous grazing, which has been the practice over nearly all our grasslands from the time of the buffalo kill off, depletes organic matter because the plants never get a chance to re-grow. When an animal is always present to eat the plant, there is little to no re-growth. This leaves the roots in a continuous pruned state and the top growth is much shorter as the roots haven't built up any reserve to feed the top growth. Organic matter is low, and cannot hold the needed moisture and nutrients the soil requires.

This is a double hit. Short roots that can't reach valuable moisture and nutrients and less moisture and nutrients available as the storage effect of organic matter has been depleted. I have read that most soils contain one half or less of the organic matter present before continuous grazing. This cycle has to be reversed before there will be any production increase.

There are several processes going on below ground at the same time. Sunlight, CO_2 and water form carbohydrates and fuel leaf growth, which when maximized, not only allows roots to store the excess for future use, but also feeds the many microbes in the soil. The nutrients made by the microbes (bacteria and fungi) are then available to the plant. Surface litter broken down by hoof action (tromping), earthworms and other small organisms begins the process of returning these nutrients to the soil for further action by the underground process.

High amounts of organic matter and carbon (organic matter is 58% carbon) not only hold water and nutrients for plant use, but will also bring soil PH towards neutral.

Research indicates neutral ph soils have the highest diversity of bacteria. The amount and diversity of soil microbes is the most important aspect of soil life. Just as micro-flora in the rumen feed the animal, soil microbes feed the plant.

Carbon sequestration in the soil is also important for increasing soil health and productivity. The essential element in building life is carbon, whether in our bodies or in the soil. Carbon holds inorganic soil particles together, while storing vast amounts of moisture. A cubic foot of soil will hold four additional gallons of water with a 1% increase in carbon. Since carbon is a component of organic matter it is returned by the same process explained above. This is a complete cycle that when properly instituted creates more energy than used, building more soil in the process.

Healthy soils build healthy plants, increasing production, which in turn supports more animals that will return more energy to the soil. This basic overview of what is going on under the surface will enable you to begin making the management changes that will bring soil to life.

I would like to quote something Kit Pharo, of Pharo Cattle Company said about 15 years ago. "You do not have to understand how a computer works to make it work." The same goes for understanding in detail all the actions going on in your soil. More importantly the manager must realize that if above ground management is correct the processes in the soil will take place even if he doesn't know exactly how it happens. As any kid would say, "Awesome!"

If you are interested in studying the exact processes taking place in building soil there are many sites available to study. You can run your own search or start with the sites I will list in the resource section. I like detail and enjoy reading the new findings that come out on a regular basis. I may complain about some of the research being done in agriculture, but not in the study of soil. This is basic research that must be done before we have the deep understanding we need to make grazing decisions.

The following pieces on grazing management will focus on the techniques needed for implementation of soil rebuilding. It is as much a mind change as it is a procedural change. Most of what has been learned or practiced in the past has to be discarded and replaced with methods that recognize the vitality of the natural world.

It is claimed to take a thousand years to make an inch of soil. That may be true when grinding a rock into fine grains suitable for soil. It may not be true when making an inch of nearly lifeless soil into a living organism. This change comes from our continual investigation of good soil and how it can be made.

The first thing to understand is that topsoil is built from the top down. It is the steady feeding with plant litter, manure and urine that makes soil. We are striving for a living soil. Soil that is the home of millions of microorganisms. This is where true fertility comes from.

I feel sure many of you have seen the pictures and videos of grass being grown on the sides of tailings ponds left over from mining operations. The material in these slopes is from deep under ground and has absolutely no life. Yet, it can be brought to life with just a little help. The really good part of this is that cattle (hated by most environmentalists) are the large organisms that provide the initial energy to begin the buildup of smaller organisms, which bring life to soil.

The procedure is to first scatter late cut hay with seed on the slopes, then put up electric fencing to hold the cattle in fairly small plots. The next step is to put a large number of cows (heavy animals work best) into a small enclosure, and let them do what comes naturally. They eat, urinate, defecate and tromp. Their tromping action presses the hay, urine and feces into the soil where it can start the process of building a microbial population when the seed from the hay sprouts and begins growing. This is natural soil building enhanced by man, which is more successful than trying to grow grass on similar slopes without animals.

My first lesson in soil building began in 1968 when I leased a neighbor's place that had a couple of small fields. Not wanting to farm, the owner and I worked out a deal to plant the fields back to grass. The larger of the two fields, 140 acres, was on a side hill. In the middle of the field were several acres of alkali that grew nothing. Although a small seep at the top of the hill kept it wet most of the year, the very top layer was dry and covered in white alkali dust all year long. A cloud of white dust would be boiling from the surface anytime the wind blew.

The owner had row crop farmed sorghum feed for his cows on this field with a small Ford tractor. Even though the alkali spot was wet, it could be crossed with the light tractor. Since the owner was row cropping and didn't want to break his rows, he continued to farm across this spot, even though it never grew anything. His crop would sprout and die. In discussing what to do with this spot, we decided it would take many years for it to become productive. We then fenced it to keep it separate from the rest of the field. I Put in a cover crop that year and planted the field to grass the next spring.

We planted blue grama, sideoats grama, and a small amount of yellow clover. I had to plant around the alkali spot, as the tractor I was using would get stuck in the wet soil. While building the fence I also picked up a lot of old junk boards, rotted wood, tree leaves and tree limbs to spread on the spot to help prevent it from blowing.

The grass in the field came up nicely and made a good stand. In a short time our lessons in the power of nature began. Surprisingly kochia weed began growing in the alkali. We did not expect anything to grow, especially this soon. The next year in addition to kochia we had blue grama, sideoats grama plus alkali sacoton from a nearby hard bottom.

We did not understand what changes took place in the alkaline soil to allow grass to come in on its own so soon, but it was obvious the process was started when farming was discontinued. (Looking back with what I now know, it is obvious the grass plants and kochia were alkali tolerant while the sorghum was not. Were microorganisms still present in this soil that had absolutely no organic matter? If not, why did the grass do so well?) The third summer along with grass, we found elm trees and tamarisks starting by themselves. By the fifth year the site was completely covered by grass and the fence was removed. There was absolutely no sign of the old alkali spot. Nature had won.

If soil can be created from junk, just think what can be done with soil that has a head start! The possibilities are endless.

I witnessed another example of soil building taking place on my ranch that further convinced me soil could be created from junk. When we began fencing for my controlled grazing, we fenced out a dug pit in one corner of a school section I leased, as it was going dry. When the pit was dug, the spoils were piled up in a long berm about 50 to 60 feet long and maybe eight feet high. The top layer of the berm would have come from 12 to 15 feet down in the pit, where there was absolutely no life

The five acre fenced area was also to be a small wildlife area. Our grazing plan was to turn the cows in once or

48

twice a year while they were in an adjoining paddock. At first it was only in the winter, but as the large bare area around the pit recovered, the cows were allowed in once during the summer also when it was past duck nesting time.

Before we fenced the pit, it was just like any other water area you have seen. Most of the five acres was grazed down and out a ways from the pit, no vegetation at all. There was a little salt grass around the base of the berm. The very first season the bare areas started re-vegetating. In three years the grass grew right to the edge of the pit.

The berm was a surprise also, as kochia weed once again showed its value as not only a forage source, but also as a soil rejuvenator. Kochia began growing on the berm, starting the soil building process. The salt grass began moving up the berm and not only began covering it, but was turning junk into living soil. The process would have been quicker if I had scattered hay to put more organic matter into the soil.

The actual reason the soil building began was the fencing that gave the needed rest to allow plants to get started and have time to become established. Previously the pit, and the pasture, had been in continuous grazing. The berm received hoof action, but no rest to allow plants to take over. The long rest period gave plenty of time for plants to recover.

Nature, on its own, except for the controlled rest, proved it was capable of again doing what it had been accomplishing for thousands of years. The lesson here is to provide a little low-level technology (the electric fence), knowledge (number of cattle, sufficient rest time and possibly organic matter to jump start the process), then stand back and let nature do its thing.

The following is a, "dirty thirties", story.

After a severe two-day dirt storm a farmer was walking around on his land surveying the damage. He came across a hat lying on the ground and picked it up. Underneath was a man! The guy told the farmer he sure was glad to see someone and asked if he could dig him out. The farmer ran to get a shovel and began digging. Just as the farmer thought he could get the guy out, he said, "Keep digging, I'm horseback!"

MY GRAZING EXPERIENCE

As with most ranchers, my grazing management was similar to what my dad and neighbors did and the ranches that I worked on after high school. A basic summer and winter pasture back and forth. Nothing complicated. Took very little thought, except to decide when to turn out in late spring or early summer.

With very little cool season grass (next to none) we had to wait for the warm season grasses to start growing.

Time To Change

Tentative turn out date was May 10th. In the spring we worried about getting through the summer, and then by mid-summer were wondering about winter. Like much of the west our annual precipitation was in the 12 to 14 inch range.

Our operation consisted of mostly leased land, with a small deeded base. In this situation we fluctuated up and down on acres of land to graze. In areas to the east we hear about land readily available, land not even grazed. This doesn't happen in Eastern Colorado. It is hard to find grass to lease and it is expensive. In the late eighties we were down to 80 cows, from 130 cows and their calves, which we always ran over as yearlings.

I decided it was time to change management to a way that I had some influence over the outcome. If I could increase production on what land I controlled and run more cows on that base, I could reduce fixed costs, lessen time and labor and also eliminate competing for more lease grass.

While reading about Allan Savory's Holistic Management in 1979, I agreed with portions of his philosophy, but had trouble with other parts. I kept studying though and gradually began to accept his thoughts. In 1982 friends, Tom and Cheryl Jolly, at Hugo, Colorado attended the Savory Holistic Management course. They then initiated the first Holistic Grazing ranch in

Colorado. After several visits with Tom and Cheryl and attending a tour of their ranch, I decided to go the next step.

After studying Savory's Holistic Resource Management book (now Holistic Management) the winter of 1988-89, it was time to get started. My first decision was how many paddocks to set up. This is a thought provoking question that has many variables to consider. The availability of water? Cost of fencing? Wagon wheel or block system? Start slow and gain experience before subdividing into more paddocks? Begin with many paddocks at the beginning? The number of paddocks and the water system are probably the most stressful decisions in getting started.

After thinking over the possibilities it became clear that that if I built a large number of paddocks it would make planning decisions simpler and lessen the chance of a blunder. If I did make a mistake, it would be much easier to correct. The final design had 24, 80-acre paddocks. The yearlings were several miles away on a very poorly watered pasture, which remained unfenced. Occasionally our horses grazed on a couple of the paddocks, but usually were on other unfenced grass.

Considering the area covered and lack of water where it was needed, the wagon wheel design was the logical choice. We did put in one mile of pipeline, but it was needed anyway whether or not we changed grazing methods. One section of land only had a dug pit in a far corner and it was nearly dry at the time. The pipeline watered a 14-pasture cell with a 20' tank in the center. Another cell was part wagon wheel, part block with 6 pastures. The final cell had four paddocks radiating from a windmill in a corner.

The majority of our posts were used cedars from a neighbor who was replacing several miles of fence. A post doesn't have to be first class for electric fences. Corner posts were cut from used oil field production tubing that also was free. This kept my fencing costs to a reasonable amount. The wire, insulators and a few fiberglass posts cost $1.40 an acre.

After deciding on the number of paddocks, the next decision was time grazed in each and time needed for recovery before coming back again. During the growing season I decided on two days in each paddock the first time through and four the second time. This two-day grazing resulted in a 46-day recovery period for the first move with 92 days for the later move.

In this area the growing season for grass was usually figured from late April to the end of August. Setting definite days would seem to be too structured for good grazing management, but we were concentrating on growing as much grass as possible for winter grazing. In the beginning I had only 80 cows going through the system, building up to 110 head in three years. I called the first pass through a, "freebie," as the amount of grass grazed in two days was not noticeable. At most, 90 to 95 pounds per acre, dry matter basis. The cows and calves gained very well with these short graze periods.

Also, even though some pastures were better than others, it was not enough to make a difference with our short number of days in a pasture and the amount of rest time. The small amount we were taking in each pass left the pastures in excellent shape. In our arid environment, with blue grama, we did not have to worry about grass growing too fast and not being in the proper stage for eating quality. Blue grama is always palatable, no matter the stage or time of year. It is very forgiving.

Going through winter with 24 paddocks required an average time of nine days in each one to make it to spring. I evaluated the grass in each paddock for probable days of grazing, taking into consideration recovery time and what I judged to be the amount of grass production. The better paddocks were assigned twelve days grazing, the average in growth nine days and the rest six days. This was adjusted to give my needed time of about nine days per paddock. The pastures were grazed down to about the same level with this variable time period.

There seems to be one aspect of controlled grazing that escapes the thinking of those still practicing continual grazing. That is the number of days of the growing season grass is grazed in the differing systems. In the continual method, grass is grazed the entire season. Grass plants do not get any rest. They are continually under stress. The plants do not have a chance to express their ability for growth.

Under controlled grazing grass and other forages get a substantial level of rest in the growing season. With my grazing plan each acre was grazed only six days in the summer. The remainder of the time it was resting, growing both leaves and roots. This makes for a healthy and productive plant. Overall my grass was grazed an average of 15 days in a year, which leaves a rest period of 350 days.

We started with about 24 acres per cow at 80 head and at 110 cows it was down to about 17 or 18 acres per head. Some ranches figured 30 or more in this area. Smaller ranches tend to hay more and keep the acres per cow down a little lower. We were able to increase cow numbers while eliminating hay. With this management we had plenty of winter grass. This was much more of an improvement than it might seem.

This paragraph is a repeat of the fourth paragraph at the beginning.

"I decided it was time to change management to a way that I had more influence over the outcome. If I could increase production on what land I controlled and run more cows on that base, I could reduce fixed costs, reduce time and labor and also eliminate competing for more lease grass."

We ran an additional 30 head for about seven years. As the grass improved we added numbers and then backed down with the beginning years of the drought to 80 again. Our one time fencing cost of approximately $2800 could easily be amortized over 20 years. That is $140 per year. Divide this by 30 and grass cost for those extra 30 cows was $4.66 per year! If I had leased more grass to run that extra 30 head it would have cost $3750. These are the figures used to arrive at that amount. At 25 acres per cow x 30 head = 750 x $5.00, the going rate for lease at the time, = $3750. Pull out your calculator and figure how much that saved us in the seven years.

A reduction in fixed costs lowers the break even for every calf sold. When you are thinking of changing your grazing management it is best to sit down with a calculator and run numbers for anything you can think of. It might take a while to see what works and what does not, but it is the only way to ease your mind, and see the possibilities.

RE-ESTABLISHING HIGH SUCCESSION GRASSES

I had two main goals when changing grazing methods. One was to increase production on grasses already present, the other was to encourage grazed out high production grasses to come back and spread.

The sandhills on my ranch, predominantly blue grama, should have been covered with higher succession warm season grasses such as sand bluestem, prairie sandreed, yellow Indiangrass and switchgrass. Depleted cool season grasses, although in smaller amounts, would be western wheatgrass, thickspike wheatgrass and needle and thread.

During the open range era of the late 1800's and/or the early homestead days, severe continuous grazing damaged large areas of Eastern Colorado. High production warm season grasses were displaced by lower production blue grama and buffalo grass. Cool season grasses that would have lengthened the grazing season nearly disappeared.

Changing the blue grama monoculture into a diversified community with tallgrasses more dominant, as they probably were at one time, would create a significant increase in overall production. The tallgrasses, with more leaf growth, also are deeper rooted, gathering up moisture from a lower level than blue grama plants. A varied and healthy root structure is very important, since water will quickly move through sand, leaching valuable nutrients.

Blue grama is a very high quality grass, but we were interested in raising production to a higher level than it could reach. A greater diversity of forages will not only increase production, but also give the grazing animal a greater variety for nutrient selection.

The high succession grasses have two to three times more production than blue grama (more on blue grama below). Also, adding one month of cool season grazing onto both spring and fall would be a significant increase.

Before more explanation on our progress, we need to look at how grasses can be killed or damaged. Grass can be very tough, but all grasses, tallgrasses especially, are vulnerable to continual grazing. The growing point of grass, the mere stem, can easily be damaged.

The mere stem rises from the crown in varying heights, depending on the grass variety. The taller the grass, the higher this growing point is elevated above ground level. Conversely the short grasses have a very low growing point. During overstocking and continual grazing the growing point of the taller grasses can easily be bitten off. When this happens too many times the plant will die. Cool season grass can be killed the same way.

This is apparently what happened in our area. There were only scattered remnants of both the high production and cool season grasses that should have been dominant over blue grama. After several years into my grass management, it was certain that reversing the trend would take many years.

This was the environment that I faced when planning my grazing management. With sufficient rest, we began finding many small patches of these grasses, such as sand bluestem, switchgrass and prairie sandreed. Cool season thickspike wheatgrass, western wheatgrass and needle and thread became noticeable. A very few sideoats grama plants were found also, but no yellow Indiangrass, which should have been present.

After finding these spots, we monitored them over the years. It was obvious most were expanding, but not at the rate I had envisioned. These grasses were there all along, but with continuous grazing they never reached a height that made them noticeable. The leaf height would have been no more than blue grama and the plant never had a chance to put up a seed head.

After we found the patches of grasses scattered around in different areas, it was evident the varieties were segregated. There was little mixing of any two at one spot. Sand bluestem was found around our small blowouts, one trail road and a sandy bottom. Bare ground and a lack of competition seemed to be important to this grass.

Prairie sandreed was not as thick where we found it, but it covered a much larger area than all the other grasses except needle and thread. Competition from blue grama didn't seem to affect it; although it didn't grow where blue grama was a tight sod.

Thickspike wheatgrass was found on a hillside that dirt had blown onto from an old field during the thirties. It gained four to six times in area, after it was found. The field, just over the break of the hill, still showed the effects of blowing with grassed humps and bare ground in between. The old field improved with the rest it was given, but looking back with the knowledge I now have, it should have been fenced into small enclosures. A much better response would have been obtained with the severe trampling of a large number of cows.

Needle and thread made quite a comeback, spreading over a hundred acres or more, but once again, mostly in one area. It seemed to have survived by growing under sagebrush, as that is where it was first found.

Switchgrass was found only in isolated clumps that spread little if at all. That seemed odd since we hand seeded switchgrass in bare spots and had great results. Western wheatgrass also seemed to make little progress through the years.

No tallgrasses were found anywhere there was a tight sod of grama. There was just too much competition. Tall-grasses established in thin sod were spreading although not as fast as in bare spots.

Another problem covering a large portion of eastern Colorado is blue grama changing from a bunch grass to a sod type grass. Where blue grama is still a bunch type it is much more productive than the sod type. Even though the growing point of blue grama is low, intense continual grazing still damaged the plant and for survival it turned into a sod forming plant.

It is assumed that a high level of hoof impact can make changes. I tried scattering grass seed around my salt and mineral troughs when putting cattle in a new paddock. If the grass was thin or there was a bare spot it was successful. There was no response in heavy blue grama sod, even if the grass was trampled down to the crown.

Whether this situation be remedied or how long might it take was a big, "IF." In the mid 1990's, Tom Jolly, early Holistic Management practitioner, arranged a meeting of ranchers involved in controlled grazing to assess this situation. A definite solution was not settled on, as there were no clear cut ideas to work from even after a lengthy discussion.

One rancher said we needed to keep doing what we were doing, no matter how long it took. Another thought we should try to speed up the process, saying there was a difference between, "geologic time and bankers time!"

"We make a living by what we earn-we make a life by what we give."

Winston Churchill

SAND SAGEBRUSH
WHY CUSS IT? GRAZE IT?

As you travel through the sandhill country of Eastern
Colorado it is evident sand sagebrush is a definite part of
the landscape. It can vary from almost none to relatively
thick. Individual plants can vary from small to well over
two feet tall. Unlike some sages, cattle readily eat sand
sagebrush. That is, unless you baby them so much they
never have to.

In most areas of the country there are plants waiting to be
added to the list of forages cattle will eat and do well on.
Why are they not grazed? Here are a few of the reasons.
"We take good care of our cows so they will produce." "I
didn't know cattle would eat them?" "Neighbors would say
I was abusing my cows." "They are poisonous." "They
have a bitter taste that cows don't care for"." My cows
don't have to eat weeds, because I take care of them like I
should." "Only goats will eat brush." "Why should my
cows eat all that junk?" "I didn't know they contained any
nutrients?" "They're just weeds!"

In reality, not a legitimate reason in the above list. Even
toxic plants can be good food. In my title I ask why cuss it?
In the sandhills it is common for ranchers to complain
about the sagebrush taking moisture away from grass and
in some places it can be very dense and crowd the grass.

I knew that old timers in our country had relied on sagebrush for a feed source when it snowed. In the modern era cattle grazed it some, but not to the extent it had been used. Reading Allan Savory's book, "Holistic Resource Management", convinced me to make several changes and putting an end to haying my cows was high on the list.

After making the mind switch, (the hard part) it was easy to implement. Just quit! Overall it was a success, but with a problem at the beginning that had me wondering. The first winter, (1990) I was feeding the large alfalfa cubes, (about two inches square) for protein. When the first good snowstorm came along I watched the cows, but did not give in and hay. I did lose two older cows to compaction, which caused some worry, but I didn't make any changes.

The next summer at the Eastern Colorado Experiment Station at Springfield, Colorado I related this to Dr. Larry Rittenhouse of Colorado State University. He said the cows didn't have enough protein in the rumen to digest the sagebrush. His recommendation was to feed a couple pounds of cottonseed cake to feed the micro-flora in the rumen. This would enable the rumen bugs to do a better job of breaking down the sagebrush. Although it may be difficult to extract, a winter sample of my sagebrush tested 6.9% protein.

The next winter I made the switch to cottonseed cake and had no more problems. Several years later a sunflower seed oil plant was built at Goodland, Kansas. I asked Dr. Rittenhouse if sunflower protein would work also.

He said it would and I then switched to sunflower supplement at about one third the cost of cottonseed.

   With little cool season grass in this area we were without an early source of green grass. It would be late April before warm season grasses started to grow and into May before there was enough growth for grazing. Sand sage greened up earlier than warm season grasses and was grazed readily by cattle in this early stage. Later, as the grasses came on, foraging sagebrush declined.

   One thing I learned when revising my grazing management was the change in what I looked for when in the pasture. Before, I concentrated on the health of the cattle and the water supply. I would note grass condition somewhat but not in detail. Occasionally I may observe what they were eating, but, their condition was my main focus.

   After the change, I concentrated on the grasses and forages. Cows took a back seat, except for paying more attention to what they were eating, which took on importance.
Since I had not watched what cows were eating as closely before stopping hay feeding, as after, I didn't have a really good reference point to work from when comparing sagebrush grazing. I did have a strong feeling that there was quite a difference though. Of course snow cover dictated heavy usage, but it appeared there was more season long winter use. Grazing of sagebrush during spring green up may not have been much more than before.

Summer use also improved and occasionally late in the summer when calves were eating more grass, I would see one nipping at sagebrush. After several years of my cows eating sagebrush I began to feed less protein. One reason was cost, but also the experience I had with the cow noted in an earlier piece that did not eat cake, but stayed in the herd until 9 or 10 years old. If one can, they all should.

At the reduced level of protein, even the older cows had no problems with grazing sagebrush. I believe the rumen micro flora had adjusted to sagebrush with the yearlong grazing. This led me to believe a cow is much more capable than we credit her. Let a cow be a cow!

There are other positives for sagebrush. In sand, nutrients are easily leached below the root zone of grasses, but since sagebrush is deep rooted, it will grab these nutrients for growth. When the sagebrush leaves fall of during the winter these nutrients are returned to the grass plants for use. Sagebrush will also keep wind from directly hitting the ground, slowing down evaporation.

Another factor favorable for sagebrush is the amount of blowing snow it can capture, especially in a blizzard with extremely high winds. The only snow remaining on the prairie might be what is behind the sagebrush clumps. Sagebrush will also scavenge water that has moved down past the root zone of grasses. Sagebrush will always green up, even in the worst drought years. This assures an increased amount of forage for the given availability of moisture.

Whether good years or bad, sagebrush and other plants will increase your potential for profit. Ignoring all the available forage on your land is akin to losing part of your ranch.

THE ENDURING WEED

Weeds are like mice and flies. They will always be here. No force known will eradicate them. Weeds are considered villains of the worst sort. Absolutely no good according to literature from chemical companies, who have gotten rich in this fight.

Is it true weeds are completely unworthy of sharing land with grasses and other productive forages? Partially, but in many instances weeds have a place in our environment. That goes against the grain and needs explanation. When something has been propagandized for so long it takes time to replace that thought with logic.

There are several things to know about weeds before explaining how to handle them. Weeds are natures' way of covering up bare spots due to grass damage. Any environmental damage will allow weeds to flourish. We must realize weeds are always here or they wouldn't be able to take over when given the chance. They are a natural segment of the environment. Although we have many imported alien weeds they can usually only establish themselves when man does something wrong. A good, healthy covering of grass will seldom let a weed germinate and grow.

Most weeds have good food value. Many are high in protein, which make them acceptable in a grazing system that utilizes all forages present. They are a good alternative cow feed at all times, but especially so during dry years. Weeds are generally green and growing during drought because their taproots gather moisture and nutrients below grass root level. This also is part of their survival mechanism.

Kochia and Russian thistle (tumble weed) have been especially popular in some areas for hay. Kochia is claimed to be comparable to alfalfa and grows naturally in wheat fields after harvest on the plains. Kochia was nearly the only feed my cows saw most winters because it was cheap.

Some year's kochia wasn't plentiful, but Russian thistle always was. It never failed. This plant was cussed since it appeared in South Dakota in 1873, but without it, many more cows would have starved during the dirty thirties. I'm not advocating growing Russian thistle, since I have spent many days rebuilding fence after a big blow when miles of fence was laid flat on the ground. But, if it is there, take advantage of the nutrients before they blow away.

The observation from most people is that cattle won't eat noxious weeds. The common thought is that goats must be introduced to do the work cows refuse to do. This is not true, but the word hasn't got around yet to most cattlemen that cows will readily eat weeds thought to be only goat fodder.

Various ranchers who have changed their grazing management say cows have learned to eat Canada thistle when concentrated on smaller areas. Teaching cows to eat unfamiliar plants can accelerate this behavior. Doing so brings more efficiency to the operation by using a greater percent of forage grown on the land. Also, the given amount of rainfall on the land is put to greater use when every plant is eaten.

In June 2009, I attended a program put on by Kathy Voth, of Landscapes for Livestock, who teaches cows to eat weeds that cattle seldom do on their own. This was very interesting as she explained the loss of available forage by not grazing weeds. They are there so why not take advantage of them. Although weeds are thought of as junk, they contain high nutrient values, which makes them comparable to most grasses.

I will use some of Kathy's comments from her website.

"All foods high in nutrients taste better than those high in toxins."

Then she goes on to say, "all plants contain toxins, but this doesn't make them toxic unless the dose is high."

"Animals learn to limit how much they eat of a toxic plant by mixing in other plants in their diet."

"Like us, animals sometimes do not want to try something strange."

These are the keys Kathy used in figuring out her method of teaching cattle to eat weeds.

1. Animals learn what to eat

2. They are more likely to eat nutritious foods.

3. Weeds are very nutritious.

Here are a few of the weeds she has taught cattle to eat:

Canada thistle, Distaff thistle, Italian thistle, Leafy spurge Purple starthistle and Spotted knapweed

Cows have the ability to pick and choose from various forages to attain the balanced diet her body requires. This would have been a natural process thousands of years ago when she had to live off the land. Man brought that to an end when he started babying cows by hauling hay and supplement to her and modifying behavior.

The most common method of attacking weeds is with chemicals, but this is a losing battle. No weed has ever been eliminated by chemicals. Negative. This is only a temporary fix and adds more chemicals to an already overloaded environment. Negative. Chemicals are not only expensive, but plants are becoming resistant to those now in use. Negative. This means new and more expensive chemicals must be produced, that will in turn be only temporary. Negative.

A much rosier picture emerges from grazing the pesky byproducts of improper grazing. Grazing weeds puts weight on the animal. Positive. The removal involves tramping the litter, which begins the process of building organic matter in the soil. Positive. The soil surface is in better condition for natural reseeding and/or rejuvenation of the native plant source. Positive. Better usage of available rainfall. Positive. It is cheaper. Only management is needed. Positive. Grazing is beneficial to the environment. Positive. This is a natural process, proven over thousands of years. Positive.

Teaching animals to eat unfamiliar plants requires an understanding of animal behavior. Kathy began her work by studying research by Dr. Fred Provenza of Utah State University who has been researching animal behavior for many years. His research focused first on why certain weeds, brush and other forages weren't eaten, before determining methods to teach them.

One of Dr. Provenza's proven points is that the best teacher is the animals' mother. If the mother is taught, she passes this knowledge down to her daughter through observation and when that daughter becomes a mother, it is passed down again. This ensures the knowledge is carried on to future generations. More on Dr. Provenza in THE BEHAVE PROGRAM.

Kathy's understanding of animal behavior guided her design of methods to teach cattle to eat weeds. She has developed simple training techniques that work very well. Nothing elaborate or complicated. Kathy's first method was used in pens. This learning experience led her to pasture training at a later date. In the pen method a number of cattle were penned for a seven-day period. Half-barrel tubs were placed in a pen. Feed such as alfalfa was fed to get the cattle started. Then alfalfa or some other nutritious feed was mixed in the tubs with the target plant, which has been hand picked previously (hand gathering the plant is the hardest part).

After this session the cattle were ready to go back to pasture. They then readily ate the offending weed. The classroom animals went into the herd and became unknowing teachers. While they were eating weeds, others observed and began eating the weeds. Cows are apparently very good observers of what others are eating. We don't realize how much is going on out there in the pasture. It is assumed the cow just goes out and fills her belly, then lies down to chew her cud.

Far from it. She is using a built in feed back mechanism to select a diet mixture that will provide her needed level of

71

nutrients. This is another example of letting a cow be a cow. She knows her business better than we do, so let her teach us. As we learn from her, it allows us to tweak certain things to her advantage without damaging the well-designed behavior and sense of survival.

After learning more about cattle behavior, Kathy began pasture training.

This is her explanation of the pasture method.

"The emphasis of the training is getting them over their fear of new foods and get them interested in trying lots of new foods. I do this by giving them experience with unfamiliar, nutritious foods-just bags of feed from the local co-op, like wheat bran, alfalfa pellets, different grains, etc. I feed morning and afternoon for four days and in short order they get the idea that every time I come, I'm bringing them something good, even if it looks and smells strange."

"On the fifth day I give them the weed with something they have already tried. By the third day of weed feeding they are eating it plain and I send them on to a trial pasture where they can practice grazing on their own."

To make pasture training easier she uses a cake feeder when she can. The impressive thing of her procedure is that it is SIMPLE and effective at the same time. And the cattle continue learning to eat other things as the fear of trying something strange has been eliminated. Can't get much better than this.

Compare this system to loading up a sprayer, filling it with water, mixing expensive chemicals with all the hassle and labor involved, plus knowing you will have to do this on a continual basis and wondering when will the weeds become resistant. Is this an intelligent method? No, and especially not when a cow will do it free and return a profit while she is at it!

While I was looking through Kathy's website I went to "Overcoming our Brush Prejudice." Down a ways I found she uses a term I do also, but in different words. She says,

"If one cow can do it, every cow can." I say, "If one can, they all should."

Kathy also said, "it is easier to train cows to eat weeds than teach ranchers to run goats."

"You can never go wrong investing in yourself."
Orie Voth, Kathy's dad.
This is one to think about. Increase your knowledge and use of management. A cheap investment, with large rewards.

"What is the use of living if not to strive for nobler causes and to make this muddled world a better place for those who will live in it after we are gone.

"Winston Churchill

73

WILD GRAZING WAS NOT PERFECT

One of the big mind blocks of people considering planned grazing is the bunching up of large numbers of cattle on relatively small pastures. This is so foreign to those used to spreading out cattle in large pastures that it prevents them from understanding the concept. This leads to a fear of failure in attempting such a big change.

Their mental picture of a pasture with the number of cattle involved will look like the trampled out area around a tank or loafing spot. The difference between a few cattle over a long length of time as opposed to a lot of cattle for a short period is hard for them to comprehend. The value of rest is a hard one to grasp.

The required planning and monitoring involved has worried some that they will make big blunders, which could lead to failure. Mistakes will be made, but this is common in the early stages of change in grazing management. It is reversible though, and made easier by the mind work that is the foundation of the method.

The grazing changes that are gradually becoming accepted in this country are based on the migratory movements of wild animal herds. This includes those still carried out in Africa and the historical buffalo herds of the plains. The significant part of the movements was the severe grazing and hoof action of the herds, followed by a rest period that allowed full re-growth of the grasses.

Antelope, deer and elk are mentioned in the numerous writings and books about buffalo, but no emphasis placed on their movements throughout the year. Were they an integral part of the herds, or did they go their own way at times of the year? There are many references to buffalo, deer and antelope grazing the nutritious new growth of burned areas, which was a normal occurrence.

Antelope, deer and elk also would have taken advantage of the new tender re-growth after a buffalo herd moved through taking off all old top growth and severely trampling the soil. This would be more common than grazing the fire burned grasses, as it was constant. It is normal behavior for animals to seek out the most nutritious plants for their consumption. Using this model, it might seem the smaller animals may have followed the buffalo herds much of the time. But with information from Ian Mitchell-Innes of South Africa, that may be somewhat in doubt. He said several smaller species did follow the large animals when migrating while others were territorial and didn't migrate.

Much of this is conjecture, but what I want to bring out in my meandering account, is that there may have been a tremendous amount of grazing of new growth before the plants had fully recovered. This is detrimental in the short term, but over the long haul the plants survived and prospered.

Since wild grazing was erratic, rather than planned, don't allow fear of mistakes stop you from making a change to better grazing management. Study the interaction between plants, animals and soil. Soil is the most important as without it the plant wouldn't be there for the animal to graze, which lets the plant revitalize the soil. Soil is the basis of all life and that is what we must concentrate on.

There are those that say we cannot do better than nature, but in two ways we can. With regulation of movement through fencing, water sources and knowledge of proper rest periods, we have better control over grazing than the random movements of wild animal herds. We also can sell animals during a drought instead of letting them die as they would in nature.

Planned grazing is a mental and physical journey with many detours, adjustments, modifications, and then, moments of pure satisfaction. During this journey there will be times when you will make mistakes and wonder how bad is it going to be. Don't worry; we have all been there.

CLIMAX SPECIES

During a 2004 plant discussion on a certain site revolving around climax species composition this post from Julie Elliott, NRCS Rangeland Management specialist at Wray, Colorado brought several things to light.

"There are plant species still viewed as 'climax'- those which make up the final 'mix' of species found on site that has had the best treatment (both from mother nature and man). Imagine a place that has never seen man's influence and the plants that might be there - this is the concept of climax. Climax is never a monoculture."

"This concept has been the crux of plant ecology (and correspondingly the animal community that lives there) until really recently. Now we have had enough time studying plant communities to realize that the concept of a steady state complex condition probably doesn't exist in nature. This is simply because nature is not a steady state place - drought, flood, fire, open winters, winters buried in snow, cool summers, hot summers, herds of animals coming through, no herds of animals coming through, disease, etc, etc, are constantly changing the place in which plants live. While there are plants better adapted to a particular site's variability, a long stretch of anything will ultimately change the mix of plant species living in that place to those better adapted to that particular condition."

"AND there are very few places (if any) on this earth where man has not exerted his influence, so the fallacy of saying we know what should be there (without man's influence) is all to evident."

One time my wife Judy and I were at the bank to borrow some money. When the banker, Joel, was filling out the paperwork, he said, "Oops, I started to put your account number down for the date. That would have been the year three million something." I said, "That's okay, we'll try to pay it off before then." Thought he would fall out of his chair laughing.

Chip Hines

I'm usually bothered when I make a mistake, but a friend, Carl Bloder, had a saying that helped. He would say, "In a hundred years no one will know the difference."

Chip Hines

MOB GRAZING

I suppose you could call mob grazing an intense version of planned grazing. Officially it is Ultra High Density Grazing, which puts a very large number of cattle in a very small paddock for a short duration, which is then given a long recovery time.

The purpose of mob grazing is to take off a certain amount of grass by grazing, and then tromp the rest onto the ground. The hoof action of laying the uneaten plant (litter) down onto the surface allows microbes at ground level to begin working. As this mat of litter is broken down, it is gradually worked into the soil where it is further digested by even more underground microbes.

This litter, although looking like a waste of plants that could be eaten, has to be returned to the soil for increased fertility. The mind has to make a jump OVER what we previously thought to be correct to accept this method. The more litter the better. After only a couple of years in high a rainfall area or on irrigated land, this method generates a tremendous increase in production. A corresponding increase in plant growth follows every increase in litter. And this plant growth increase is by management only with no added fertilizer.

Can mob grazing be used anywhere? That is still to be decided. There are logistic problems to be solved in many T areas. Low rainfall areas present another set of unknown problems. The method will have to be adapted to each environment, each ranch, each management style and ranch goals. There will be many that will not attempt this method because of the need for more management, more planning, more fencing and faster moves. Not everyone will feel the need go to this level to be successful.

This high level of litter recycling gives a tremendous boost to the microbial production that is actually creating the underground fertility. The how to of mob grazing is to increase the stock DENSITY on a piece of land. Stocking rate is the acres needed to run a cow for a year. Stock density is the pounds of animals on a certain size piece of land.

This is may be a little hard to comprehend at first, but with some explanation it will become understandable. First we need to assume the size animal and stocking rate before going any further.

We will begin with 100, 1000-pound cows with five acres needed to run one cow for one year. These are dry cows to simplify the math. The five acres is determined from a take half, leave half rate. At this rate we will need 500 acres of pasture. This would require 1.37 acres per day (500 ÷ by 365 days) to keep the cows in feed for one year. If the cows are moved an average of every five days the stock density would be 14,599 pounds per acre.

This is how it is figured. The acres needed for a five day move is 1.37 X 5, which is 6.85 acres. 100 cows X 1000 pounds is 100,000 pounds. Divide this by the acres needed in a five-day move. 100,000 pounds ÷ by 6.85 is 14,599 pounds per acre.

Now let's go to one move every 24 hours. This would be 1.37 acres per day. The stocking rate is the same, but density is going up by shortening time and area. Divide 100,000 by 1.37 and the stock density is 72,993 pounds per acre. If half-day moves were implemented density would double to 145,986 pounds. Stocking rate never changes in these calculations.

As you can see when time and area are shortened, density goes up dramatically. By increasing density this puts more pressure of movement on the cattle when eating in a small area, which gets more hoof action to lay down plants and tromp them into the soil. This greatly increases microbial action, which is the mainstay of increasing fertility and bringing life to your soil.

Although the reason for mob grazing is to increase stocking rate, Ian Mitchell-Innes of South Africa, a Certified Holistic Management Educator and mob grazing instructor, recommends increasing density first, with what would be a normal stocking rate for the land. This is to allow the soil time to increase in fertility and soil life before adding more cattle (stocking rate).

Ian was able to not only increase cattle numbers on his ranch during a recent drought, but even then didn't use all his ranch acreage. This was due to two things. One, Ian had been mob grazing for a time and this had greatly increased the microbial activity and fertility of the soil. Two, this also vastly expanded the soil's water holding capacity. A much larger amount of water was captured and retained in the soil. This retention enabled the plant to continue growing while in neighboring soil the plants had stopped growing for lack of water.

Capturing and retaining water is often not considered as important as other things, but without sufficient water, none of the other above and below ground systems will be as efficient. This is a far-reaching benefit, as it not only works in good times, but bad times as well. Everything involved in the soil-plant relationship is important. The highest efficiency is obtained when each part is working with the other.

Did you know?

The French company that made the statue of liberty also made small replicas for sale in the United States. The name of the company was Gadget`. Of course few here realized the T was silent so it was pronounced Gadget. The rest is history.

SHORTGRASS MOB GRAZING

I have some concerns with applying mob grazing to typical Eastern Colorado shortgrass country. I believe it can be done, but it will take significantly more thought, planning and monitoring than in tallgrass areas. In a predominantly blue grama shortgrass prairie total production ranges from 900 to 2,000 pounds per acre. This doesn't give much to work with compared to a tallgrass situation.

The Colorado shortgrass regions receive 10 to 16 inches of precipitation with a 25 to 50 acre stocking rate. Cutting this much land into small pastures to increase animal impact will be a challenge. Pipelines are expensive and long water lanes may make design and operation difficult. In wet areas where many cattle can be run on small acreages, far fewer feet of pipeline or water lanes are needed. Solving the water problem will be the very first item to tackle, and the most expensive. Because of environment, topography, location of wells, soil type, personal preference and numerous other variables, there seldom will be two systems alike.

Next is the height of the grass being grazed? In shortgrass country the total height in a growing season is usually four to five inches or less. In tallgrass country it is easier to graze the top part of the plant and leave the rest to be trodden down. When the plant is four inches tall, nearly all is taken in one bite! In tallgrass country a percent of the plant can be grazed as the animal eats from the top down leaving the lower part to trample onto the ground while moving from plant to plant.

The shortgrass grazier will have to either leave cattle in a paddock only long enough to let the cattle graze a certain percentage of plants, or leave them long enough to eat every plant. By taking only a percent of plants, there may not be enough hoof action to tromp the remaining plants into the soil. More hoof action will come from eating every plant, but will leave only small amounts of litter to put back on the ground.

I believe this problem may have an answer in the study of buffalo movements. Although some modern researchers claim there is a possibility some buffalo herds didn't have a yearly migration, it is still accepted fact and this fits in with my thoughts on how the study of their movements and mob grazing may work. By no means have I read everything published on buffalo, but enough to get a general idea of their behavior.

The huge size of the herds grazing across the prairies is hard to imagine, even if they weren't exaggerated, which I am sure they were to some extent. Almost every plant would have been eaten to ground level, if not tramped down. The depth and width of these herds meant severe hoof action and the pressure on plants would have been tremendous.

The big herd movements were seasonal so the buffalo weren't always in massive herds. At times of the year they were spread out over large areas in smaller groups moving the same direction. Grazing in this type of behavior may have left strips of un-grazed grass. May, as I am doing some guessing here.

There are numerous accounts of buffalo on the move, running for hours according to many stories. While on the move all forage would have been tromped into the soil. Nothing spared. Each of these movements, whether huge grazing herds, spread out grazing or running, would leave behind a different pattern of plant use; from all eaten, to all tromped in, to possibly a strip pattern. This patchwork of alternating destruction and un-grazed grass would probably be different the following year. With varying usage and a year or more to recover it stimulated recovery and total growth. Grazing by other animals would have caused some disruption of this as a perfect model, but then nature never has been perfect. One thing to note is that over large time frames there was a kind of equilibrium derived from the grazing or most these animals would have disappeared.

I will add another thought that I have seen no information on, and that is whether buffalo followed a set migration path. I am going to say no, but they may have hit certain areas every year because of known water availability. Other areas may have been grazed only when rains had filled waterholes.

If differing environmental forces changed their general direction, some regions may have had a two-year or longer re-growth period, which would allow the severely abused grasses time to recover fully. Another factor affecting recovery time would be the estimated number of buffalo, which ranges from a low of 15 million to a high of 50 million. This is a huge discrepancy. Drought would have made large changes in herd numbers as they would be up during the flush years and then drop in the drought years. The old and young would not survive and cows would be open, bringing numbers back to a sustainable level until the drought broke, starting a new cycle of increasing numbers.

Now back to my thoughts on how to plan mob grazing in the shortgrass environment. I had been struggling with this until reading something Terry Gompert, Nebraska Extension Educator, had written and also his comments at the Kearney Grasslands Conference.

Since a cow grazing in short grass will take off most of the plant instead of a portion, the paddock must be designed to make the cows travel more and tromp down a lot of grass as she is foraging. A long narrow paddock would encourage more travel and hoof action among the cows. The same amount might be grazed as in a square paddock, but with increased hoof action due to the differing paddock shapes.

I previously had been opposed to water lanes, but I can now see an advantage if done right. During a report of a pasture walk in South Dakota, Terry Gompert pointed out the best response to hoof action was in the water lane. That makes sense because of the high level of cattle movement in the lane. If this lane could be temporary and moved each year it would stimulate more land for the greatest improvement.

In a low rainfall blue grama situation a full years rest would be required. Paddocks and moves could be designed to give a certain number of paddocks a two-year rest. Over a span of years, each paddock would have a turn at the two-year rest period.

I think the main point in shortgrass grazing is that a high level of hoof action is more important than how much is removed. In most cases the plant will be grazed very short, but if it gets heavy tromping and plenty of rest it should be invigorated. This would be especially true in sod bound blue grama. It needs relentless tromping in a short time frame.

In the beginning a one-year rest period could be used, then as production improved, a two-year rest would be used instead of adding cattle until production is sure to hold increasing numbers. The sod bound blue grama prairie

needs a complete transformation if production is to be
raised significantly.

If sand sagebrush is present, the sagebrush could be the
signal plant to key on. If taken down very short, recovery
time can be three years or more. A certain amount of
growth should be removed, but not so much as to inhibit re-
growth. This will take some experimenting for the proper
removal amount. Since sand sagebrush is deep rooted,
growth will be more consistent, even in dry years. Every
plant needs to be thought of as a grazing resource that can
be blended into the grazing management plan.

I apologize for my meandering thinking on this subject. It
may take years of trial and error to formulate a general
direction and then revising to adjust to local environmental
conditions. Since shortgrass prairies cover such a large area
in several states we need to encourage more experimenting
to devise a strategy to bring this land back to full
production.

One thing I am sure of is that it will be resolute
individuals out there on the land doing the hard work and
ignoring those who say they're fighting a hopeless battle.

Whether my ideas will work or not, doesn't matter as
much as giving a starting direction for far ranging,
passionate discussions amongst those who don't fear
change, and look forward to the mind stimulation it brings.

FARMING & ANIMALS

In July, 2009 Kevin Fulton of Litchfield, Nebraska sent several photos to a discussion site of his cattle eating in a weed-infested field. Kevin said in the summer of 2008 he had so much rain that he couldn't get into the field to do any farming and the weeds took over.

Instead of using chemicals, as his neighbors do, to kill weeds, he grazed down the weeds using Ultra High density grazing. Kevin fenced the cattle in small breaks to obtain the maximum pounds removed from the land. The focus was more on clearing the weeds for ground preparation than leaving a heavy mat of litter.

After the cattle were removed, Kevin disked the field once, and then planted winter wheat. Summer of 2009 the wheat averaged 80 bushels to the acre. Across the fence a field that was farmed conventionally, with fertilizer and chemicals, made 45 bushels to the acre.

The chemicalized and fertilized and over tilled field had a large input cost to recapture before any profit could be realized. Kevin's field furnished valuable gain to his cattle before being farmed once and planted, with no added inputs. How can you beat a system like that?

THE BEHAVE PROGRAM

While I discount certain university and USDA research projects, there are some that have a direct and valuable application to profitability on the ranch. The BEHAVE program of the Wildland Resource Department at Utah State University, headed by Dr. Fred Provenza, is one that needs more exposure and adoption. BEHAVE stands for, Behavioral Education for Human, Animal, Vegetation and Ecosystem.

This research delves into the behavior of animals and how we can better understand them to improve forage utilization while improving our environment. Humans must understand the dynamics of animal behavior before transforming their own thought processes. This will enable people to work with animals instead of unknowingly holding them back. We must accept animals as our direct connection to the land and any additional improvement over the norm will only begin with our knowledge of their behavior.

This is from the BEHAVE site.

"Behavioral principles can provide solutions to problems by producers and land mangers. Unlike the infrastructure of a ranch such as corrals, fences and water development,

90

behavioral solutions often cost little and are easily transferred from one situation to the next. Unfortunately, we often ignore the power of behavior to improve systems.

As animals grow and develop, their interactions with the environment shape their behavior. Experiences early in life are especially critical in shaping behavior, but these interactions continue throughout life. Thus, the issue isn't if animals adapt to changes in their environment-they do every day of their lives. The only question is whether or not people want to be part of that process."

Obtaining high production from our land takes more than just putting an animal in the pasture. Over many thousands of years a certain behavior guided the natural grazing process of animals, which made them efficient grazers. Through ignorance we have reduced that ability, which lessened the amount of production derived from the land. We must encourage animals to again make better use of all that is available for profit and environmental stability.

"Our lives begin to end the day we become silent about things that matter."

Martin Luther King, Jr.

MOVING CATTLE

'Moving' cattle may be the most misunderstood term in controlled grazing. Those not familiar with new grazing techniques envision a full-scale gather and drive to another pasture. Thinking this had to be done every few days, with no attempt to truly understand how it works, has led to ridicule of the whole method.

How to move cattle is somewhat determined by the type of pasture design you choose. Moving cattle is much easier with the wagon wheel system, as the fences come to a point at the cell center water tank. By simply opening the gate into the next pasture, the cattle will find it open when they come into water and leave in the new pasture.

Cattle in a block design can be called to a gate into the new paddock by an audio signal if they haven't already seen the person and are heading in that direction. The signal can be a referee whistle, pickup horn or the holler you use when calling cattle to feed in the winter. On one ranch I visited, the mineral tub mounted on skids, was pulled by a four wheeler with the cows following to the next paddock.

Since cattle are smarter than we give them credit for, the learning procedure for these movements is very short. They quickly learn that they are on the way to new grass and need no urging.

In my wagon wheel system I had to leave one cell center at the outer edge of a pasture to go into the next system. The first time I had to do this, of course, was in the middle of the summer. I bellered a rendition of my feed call, and amazingly, here they came. I thought that call would only work in the winter to tell'em their cake was here and they'ed better hurry. I was pleasantly surprised. Them ole' hides're smarter than I thought.

The number of cattle to be moved makes little difference, as they are always ready to go to new pasture. The cattle can be checked as they file through the gate if the moves are fairly fast. If the moves are several days apart, time is still saved when checking cattle because they are in smaller pastures and you know exactly where they are. On larger operations this saves a lot of time riding over several sections of rough country looking for cattle.

This may sound kinda' mystic, but it seemed my cows were more comfortable being in close contact instead of always spread out. I can't quite explain what I was seeing or experiencing, but I believe it was related to their herding instinct from thousands of years ago.

"I felt pretty good several days ago, but I got over it."

Leonard Tarpenning, an old cowboy (my brother-in-law)

THE LONE RANGER ANALOGY

This is a great story and clearly illustrates what we have been going through in the cattle industry.

The Lone Ranger and Tonto went camping in the desert. After they got their tent all set up, both men fell sound asleep.

Some hours later, Tonto wakes the Lone Ranger and says, "Kemo Sabe, look towards the sky, what you see?"

The Lone Ranger replies, "I see millions of stars."

"What that tell you", asked Tonto.

The Lone Ranger ponders a moment then says, "Astronomically speaking, it tells me there are millions of galaxies and potentially billions of planets. Astrologically, it tells me that Saturn is in Leo. Time wise, it appears to be approximately a quarter past three in the morning."

"Theologically, it tells me that the Lord is all-powerful and we are small and insignificant. Meteorologically, it seems we will have a beautiful day tomorrow." "What's it tell you Tonto?"

"Kemo Sabe, you dumber than buffalo poop......it means someone stole the tent!"

This illustrates how some minds can completely miss the obvious, while another clearly assesses the situation and sees the answer. Some people tend to think in terms of such elaborate reasoning that simplicity is incomprehensible. That technology and complexity holds the answer to all problems.

Ranching has been drifting in this direction for the last forty or fifty years. We have let a simple business evolve into something almost unrecognizable to the natural world it is based on. It takes a lot of discipline to ignore all the hoopla pressuring you to continue adding more inputs into your operation and making it more complicated.

It is a never-ending battle to purge the false thoughts of 'progress' from the brain and institute unadulterated simplicity. The struggle may not cease until the results of using this process are visible on the land. As one success leads to another this becomes embedded and doesn't require second-guessing. It comes naturally.

Doing a little here and a little there to make things easier for either our cattle, or us, may seem small, but all these 'little things', when lumped together, are surprisingly large and lead down the slippery slope to much larger interventions. Once started it is difficult to find a place to exit this well trodden path.

It is as if we can't help ourselves. Our natural inclination to 'do something' is guiding us and in control. Keeping everything simple needs to be the focus anytime management decisions come up. Always remember the New Zealand farmer at this time. "Always look first for a no cost solution. If one can't be found, look for something low cost. If that can't be found, step back and take a long look at the situation. It is entirely possible you don't need to make a change." Many problems are perceived as such because thinking is tied closely to technology.

Revamping thinking procedures to focus on simplicity takes time, but is absolutely necessary to lessen reliance on purchased inputs and the false assumption that 'doing more' will make a ranch profitable.

"Simplicity is an acquired taste. Mankind, left free, instinctively complicates life."
Katharine Fullerton Gerould.

A Kit Carson, Colorado rancher, Claude Merritt, once said, "The trouble with this country is there are too many normal years."

GENETICS

NATURAL RESISTANCE TO PARASITES

Ian Mitchell-Innes, South African Rancher and Holistic Management Educator wrote the following for the newsletter my daughter Mildy and I once published.

Nature is amazing with its own checks and balances that keep things on an even keel. It is only since man with technology, came along, that things started to go wrong. Chemicals have been marketed to improve individual animal performance and have cost the rancher and the environment and left the profit in the hands of the multi-national companies.

I ranch on the east side of South Africa, with large tick populations, which carry all three main tick borne diseases found in Africa. Since my Grandfather arrived on this property in 1863 various dips have been used. Arsenic, Toxifien, organo-phosphates, pyrethoids and then Amitraz to all which ticks have become resistant.

I dipped my cattle every second week and kept them tick free, but still experienced the odd case of tick borne disease in my cattle. Then disaster struck: I was losing up to 3% of my herd a month. I consulted various vets who told me that I had been too efficient and dipped my cattle too clean and that they had no immunity to tick borne diseases. I bought live blood vaccine and inoculated my whole herd, pregnant animals included. This vaccine gives the animal a mild form of the diseases and allows you enough time to treat it.

During the next two years, I only inoculated my calves. I assumed I had a sufficient tick population to naturally infect my cattle and improve immunity. I then stopped dipping and only spot treated the odd animal that had a very heavy tick load.

After seven years my herd had become totally resistant to all the diseases and I no longer had the expense of buying chemicals. Not only have my cattle built up immunity to the diseases, but also through not dipping, their ability to shed ticks (not let ticks attach themselves) has improved. I could never understand why the wild antelope had virtually no ticks on them, but the beef animal, which was grazing in the same paddock, was covered in ticks. The wild animals had never been exposed to chemicals. The conclusion was that there is a mechanism in nature whereby the animal secretes a substance, which keeps the ticks off, but because of dipping, that mechanism had become redundant and no longer functioned.

I noted the less I dipped the fewer ticks I had (totally the opposite to conventional thinking) and all the tick predators, such as Red Billed Oxpeckers and spiders came back to the ranch. I now cull tick taxis (I really like this term) (my dad called lice infested cows, lice carriers, but maybe this should be lice limo's) and every year there are fewer and fewer that need to be culled. This is selection for genetic immunity/resistance. There were no warnings on the dip drums of the effect chemicals would have on the otherinsect populations, which in turn affected the populations of birds and other animals, as they were all interdependent.

Ian Mitchell-Innes

Ian's mentioning of bird populations being diminished by chemicals brings to mind something I have wondered about. For years I have noticed that there are fewer birds of all kinds than when I was growing up in the 40's and 50's. I have no proof, other than my observations. It does stand to reason though that since chemicals kill all insects along with the target species, the food source for birds could be drastically reduced, leading to diminished populations.

I wouldn't be considered a bird watcher, but nighthawks have always intrigued me. During the heat of the day they could be seen sitting on fence posts. Many times I have been within10 to 15 feet of one and they didn't fly away. About dusk they would be hunting mosquitoes and other flying insects. While sitting on a post they have a rather squat, bulky appearance. But not when flying. They have a slim body and very slender scalloped wings. They swoop and dive in a very aerobatic search for food. Not many birds can match their agility.

The nighthawk numbers seem to be diminishing. There could be numerous reasons for this or possibly just one. Is it caused where they winter or in the summer breeding grounds, or both.

While building electric fence I found a nighthawk nest, the only one I ever saw. Nest, may be an overstatement, as the birds single egg was laid on bare sand between clumps of blue grama. No grass leaves, no scooped out depression. Loosing an insect hunter like this only adds to our lack of natural controls.

A County Agent approaches an old farmer about trying out some new techniques. "Naw", says the farmer, "even now I only farm half as good as I know how."

"If you don't know how to do something, just start and someone will come along and tell you, you're doing it all wrong."

Leonard Tarpenning

GENETIC PARASITE CONTROL
IN CATTLE

Once again we have to go back in time. Cattle would have had as much parasite resistance as present day wild animals, which made their existence possible. What we have done in the modern world is ignore natural capabilities and unwittingly began diminishing them to insignificance

Chemicals will never win the battle with parasites. Anyone disagree? Are you using chemicals? Why? I suspect because you don't realize another way exists, and all the magazine ads say you must. Parasites can be controlled by genetics, which is not only lasting, but cheaper.

Genetic progress is dependent on culling, whether by death, as it is in nature or by turning the offender into cash. If the weak don't fall by the wayside, the whole species is in trouble. We have been protecting the frail with chemicals instead of sending them to town. There is still a reservoir of genes to work with, but without someone marking the culls, they are inaccessible.

As in all the other aspects of management discussed in this book, the hard part is convincing your brain to see this in the true light and shut out the propaganda (spelled advertising). The chemical companies do not want you to even suspect there is another way.

Some parasites such as lice are much easier to control. It is obvious which ones are carriers, and you just need to trade them in for cash. There are usually just a few carriers so only a small number of cows need be sold.

Flies present a little different problem as every cow is attacked. It is noticeable that some cows attract fewer flies than others. Track those cows and mark them for saving replacement heifers if everything else is okay. This may be slow, but start anyway. A battle cannot be won without a beginning. I know of only one seedstock operator working on this problem using genetics and that is Pharo Cattle Company. Anytime a seedstock supplier is working on the same problems you are, it makes your job that much easier. Take advantage of this.

Cows with stomach worms (gastrointestinal nematodes) or (GI) are not as easy to detect, but the same culling regimen used with lice and flies is still very effective.

In 2002 I found notice of a research program at the USDA Agricultural Research Center at Beltsville, Maryland. This was a four-year project to use the host immune system to reduce GI nematodes. My daughter was able to go online and get a paper on the early stages of the work.

Time To Change

The following are selected quotes or passages from the paper.

"Early results demonstrated the bovine immune system effective in reducing the number of parasites established in the host. One exception was Ostertagia ostertagia, but even with this species, the immune system reduced transmission by reducing egg count."

"These studies indicate that it is feasible to control nematode infections by using the host immune system. Recently we have proven that host genetics plays an important role in determining if individual cattle become immune or not."

"Although the anthelminitics currently used to control the parasites are efficacious and safe, there are increasing concerns that within a very short time period such control programs will be inadequate."

"Resistance to the drugs by parasites infecting ruminants is increasing world wide."

"….. change the current perception that the economic effects of the parasites are, "normal" expenses of the livestock raising system."

"The only feasible and economically viable alternative to heavy anthelminitic usage is to use the host immune system and the diversity of the host genome to control disease severity and transmission."

"Resistance to gastrointestinal nematodes is strongly influenced by host genetics and a few genetically susceptible animals are responsible for most parasite transmission."

"Within the past year over 400 immune related genes have been identified."

"As important genes are identified, this information will allow the culling of animals highly susceptible to parasite infection, reduce the numbers of parasite eggs on pasture resulting in a concomitant reduction in anthelminitic use."

"Internal parasites interfere with nutrient digestion and absorption and decreased growth and productivity of grazing cattle. Parasites can also reduce resistance to other infectious agents, and the effectiveness of vaccinations."

One purpose of this research was to find gene markers to use in tests to identify susceptible cattle with DNA testing.

"Current estimates of the cost of GI nematodes to the American cattle industry are in the area of $2 to $8 billion dollars per year. This cost is based upon the cost of anthelminitic used each year, and on decreased productivity and growth in infected cattle."

Now for the kicker. This project ran from 2002 through 2006. That was three years ago. How many out there have heard of this research, let alone the results? I don't see many hands going up. If this was done to help cattlemen why was it not publicized? Was it because the research was just for other researchers to use? Was it to promote the researchers career by the simple act of publishing a paper? Are promotions based on publishing papers, even if they never see the light of day?

Do the chemical companies have a hand in suppressing this information? How many magazines depending on advertising revenue from these companies will have the guts to publish such research? If there was a threat to bring this to the public, rest assured the chemical companies would fight tooth and nail. They would spend untold thousands of dollars to belittle the research and deem it invalid!

While looking for information on something else I found an article in the online version of a freebie magazine about whether wormers are working? It was noted that worms are becoming resistant to the wormers now being used. A member of the laboratory at Beltsville, MD, from the previously mentioned GI nematode research, was one of several interviewed for the article. He mentioned several things that might help with the resistance problem, BUT not once was genetic resistance in cattle mentioned! Not even a hint!

Why are we paying for research that might be helpful and the researcher doesn't even acknowledge it. Well, we know the magazine lives on chemical ad sales, so it may have deleted genetic references. There could be several reasons, but the real problem is the suppressing of information.

This is speculation, but obviously something is going on. It surely isn't fully informing their readers, but that would not be illegal. Magazines have the right to set editorial policy and chose their direction.

I wonder where this leaves a government employee, and I for one, think it is negligence of duty. Surely, there are rules researchers must observe in performance of duty to fully represent their work. Of course they have no control over magazine policy, but could they refuse to work with those who only want to publish articles that further their agenda without regard to the actual situation?

I can't declare this next statement for fact, but it does fit very neatly with information contained in the USDA research paper. I was told a certain company working on a new parasite product about fifteen years ago, found that when they challenged calves with stomach worms approximately 25% would not carry the worms. They were genetically immune. Did the company advertise this? Would they cut their own throat by divulging information that would allow cattlemen to chart their own destiny? Not a chance.

There now needs to be a regularly published, easily accessed publication from the USDA research arm to allow this information to be dispensed to those who can make use of it. We cannot trust regular avenues of publication to stick their necks out, so, sad to say, we will have to add another expense to government spending to protect ourselves. But, that would be a small cost compared to the illions spent on research only for researches sake with no connection to those they are to serve.

The only way you can get relief from high input costs of fighting parasites with chemicals is to rely on nature. Genetics is long term. Chemicals are only temporary. Management is all you need, and a resolve to stick to it and not revert to the short-term tactics of chemical warfare.

Don't let a lack of knowledge about genetics keep you from making a move to the non-chemical battle against parasites. You do not need a PhD to run this program. Nature has it all figured out, so follow that model, use no chemicals and cull those that fail.

Producers must accept that most of the problems associated with cattle are genetically related, and can be controlled. Set up a strict culling program that will eliminate all   genetic problems. This can be done with management and save money at the same time. It is possible chemicals may be needed for a short time or in small doses, but not on a continual basis. There is no reason to allow those selling inputs to direct our thoughts and actions. All you are doing with chemical use is breeding a better parasite and that is the last thing that should be done.

WHAT THE HELL?

Whenever wild westies get to flowing, it seems quite a few cowboys have a story to relate about a horse and an electric fence. Usually with explosive consequences! Sometimes the cause of the violent maneuvers are known. Other times it is not apparent at the time of eruption. That was my situation. Totally unaware. Some might even say I was born that way! Oh, well.

Anyway, it all started with a bull whose amourous intentions were always ahead of the calendar. He didn't care about a certain turnout time. When he was ready, he was ready. A set date was just something man had in his mind and had nothing to do with several thousand years of natural mating.

So, the only way I could convince this bull that I had the upper hand in this battle of DNA dispersion was to not only pen him, but since his high jump was of near record height, I also had to put a hot wire a foot above the top board.

This pen was kinda' out of the way and was seldom used. A couple of months after bull turn out one spring I rode up to this pen from the pasture side. My wife, Judy, was in the yard and as I nudged my horse up to the gate to open it, she walked over to ask me something. This wasn't one of those
108

horseman gates with a lever on top like you see in all the
advertisements. And to make it more difficult, the latch was
on the opposite side. As we were visiting, I held the reins in
my right hand, leaned over the gate almost out of the saddle
and reached down to grab the latch with my left hand. All
of a sudden...

My horse was runnin' backwards about as fast as he
could run forwards, and he was a runner! He spun me out
of the saddle and I hit the ground mostly on my feet, but at
a speed a little above my limited abilities. I staggered along
barely in control of my equilibrium, taking huge steps. I
looked like one of those Olympic triple jumpers that take
those giant steps before takeoff and all the while hollering
whoa, you (*^$#%&*(), whoa!

But, that backwards run away was too much for my horse
and his back legs went out from under him and he flipped
upside down. That last jerk on the reins was just too much.
I couldn't stop. I ran into him and sprawled on his belly.
Right amongst four thrashing legs! It didn't take long to
figure out that wasn't any place I wanted to be! I slithered
over the side between a front and back leg. When my
shoulder hit the ground I rolled over and jumped to my feet,
looking at my horse and wondering, what in the hell had
gone wrong? I looked at Judy and she was standing there
with her mouth open, probably wondering the same thing.

Time To Change

I looked back at my horse for a clue. Now, this is deep
sand country and when he went over he planted the horn as
solid as any corner post you ever set. There he was, upside
down and still a runnin. Dunno which way, but he was still
runnin.

As my blood pressure got down below 400 over 200 my
brain started to function a little. I looked over to the spot
where it all started and the light went on. The fence was
still hot! As that set in, my thoughts were, "Boy, ole
dummy, someday your lack-o-memory is gonna get you in
trouble!

Copyright 2005 by Chip Hines

"Law of probability. The probability of being watched is
directly proportional to the stupidity of your act."

"Workin' behind a plow, all you see is a mule's hind end.
Workin' from the back of a horse you can see across the
country as far as the eye can see."

(Would you believe this was written by a cowboy?)

110

WHAT ARE PROFITABILITY TRAITS?

When it is time to buy a new bull, what does a commercial rancher look for? Performance such as weaning weight, yearling weight and fast gain? Pedigree? Conformation? Body type? Birth weight? Of course a bull is wanted that will make the operation more money. Nothing wrong with that. Now think a little about the above list. Are any of these items a sure bet to increase income?

The very first traits looked at are the performance figures. Stands to reason as we sell pounds and if we can increase weight it should put more money in our pocket. A much heavier weaning weight is a desired goal. But, that brings up another matter. This quest will bring a higher birthweight. This can create a severe problem after several generations as this is bred into the cowherd. Slow calving is hard on a calf. Pulling calves sets them back even more. Tremendous increase in labor.

Yearling weight is next. A high performer here will pass on genetics of larger mature weight to his female offspring. This means a bigger cow that eats more and requires more land area for the increased amount of grass she eats. Cow numbers must be decreased to keep from overgrazing on the same allotted acres.

111

Pedigree. If you are looking at stacking pedigrees of cattle with the same high performance you will be successful. This is also stacking problems.

Conformation and body type. Do you like high frame score bulls with a trim belly? They will sire cows that will need extra hay, supplement and care.

Milk. Do you want to improve the milking ability of your cows? This can be done, but at a cost. Cows require more nutrients to produce that increased milk flow, which cuts the number of cows that you can run on your allotted acres. These cows also need a higher nutrient level even when not lactating.

What do you think? Casts a different light on the subject doesn't it? How many people even think about the things listed above as having negative aspects? If they were it was seldom considered as most thought this was part of the cost to get the wanted high performance. These are not usually in the thought process, but need to be because they are factual! These negative effects have gradually diminished net profit without much fanfare. In reality, almost unnoticed.

Now for the other side. When looking for a new bull there are traits to look for that genuinely make more money or save money, which has the same effect on your bank account. Some are subjective traits, in which someone decides a value, while others can be derived from records and measurements.

The only mainstream seedstock producer that I know is actually marketing money making traits is Pharo Cattle Company of Cheyenne Wells, Colorado. As Kit Pharo began developing his breeding philosophy he realized performance wasn't everything. Early on was the realization that large frames, big cows and heavy weaning weights were not profitable. These cows were not as efficient as smaller frame, moderate weight cows. That led the way to other thoughts on what the commercial rancher needed for a profitable operation.

A necessary goal for profitable ranches is getting a high percent of cows bred with the least possible cost. Since fertility is a low heritable genetic trait there has been little emphasis on breeding for it. This was ignored by seedstock producers who touted fertility, although it was ' feed bucket' fertility. Kit approached this from a different direction by applying known facts.

A thin cow will not breed. A cow with a certain amount of fat cover will breed and deliver a calf. Kit decided to give the low heritability of fertility a boost and easy fleshing cows were the answer. This trait could readily be passed on through his bulls, lessening customer costs to get a cow bred.

This began a thought process of looking at other problems and evaluating what could be done to improve traits that would continually improve the profit of PCC bull customers. From this model Kit developed the star system to rate the various traits valued by PCC. In Kit's system, traits have a rating from one to five stars with five being the best. I will list the traits listed in the PCC bull sale catalog and give my personal reasons what each can do to improve profit.

Frame: Frame size is a big factor in mature weight. Large frame cows are heavier which means they need more feed through the winter to compensate.

Conversely, small frame cows weigh less. A limited number of acres of pasture will run more small cows than large cows. More calves to haul to sale barn.

Calving ease: More calves on the ground to sell. Calves that come easy get off to a better start, thus making more money. The decreased level of labor has a value. Think about it! Much less stress! Hard to put a value on this. Ask your wife. She will tell you.

Disposition: Easy handling cattle gain better. Decrease labor by huge amounts. Lower your stress level. Long overlooked.

Fleshing ability: An easy fleshing cow will breed back readily. She can get by with little or no hay or supplement for winter. Backfat is her supplemental winter feed. Huge saving in your biggest out of pocket costs. Hay and supplement expense can be the difference between a profit or loss. Once again less labor and add lower fuel cost. Leave the feed truck parked.

Hair coat: A slick haired cow has a functioning endocrine system. Fewer parasite problems. More fertile. A good doing cow requires little care. Saves labor. Reduces stress. Hers and yours.

Udder: Not ever having to milk out a cow or help her calf suck is another big labor saver. Calves get off to a better start and do better all through life. Stress saver for the cow, the calf and you!

Longevity: Another labor and money saver. She doesn't need your help. Proven fertility. Proven moneymaker. What value can you put on not having to replace a cow until she is 15 years old instead of 10?

Go through these traits and place a monetary value on what they can do for you. Much of the emphasis is on savings, which equates to a much-improved profit any way you look at it. Decreased feed costs are the biggie, but don't ignore labor savings. Use this time to do something that makes money!

All of the above points are completely ignored by mainstream seedstock producers that have a focus on performance only. They have no concept of how to truly improve the commercial ranchers profit. Rating and promoting the subjective traits has proven to be very popular with PCC customers. Commercial producers are now realizing the direction to profitability is more than performance. The high percentage of repeat customers at PCC sales is proving this philosophy.

The star traits go against the grain when performance is discussed, but we are in an era when everything must be looked at in a different light. We must question everything we do, and look for things in plain sight that have been overlooked or considered to trivial to have economic importance.

When asked by one of his Parliament members why he believes so much in America, British Prime Minister Tony Blair replied, "A simple way to take measure of a country is to look at how many want in and how many want out."

Over the years I have noticed that gossipy incidents, which were noteworthy at one time, fade away as the decades slide by. Very seldom do the much younger generations ever hear of these.

Chip

A COW CANNOT BE REDESIGNED!

The title may come as a shock to the seedstock breeders continually trying to make a cow do what they want, and not what the cow is capable of doing. The high performance campaign is focused on forcing cattle to conform to a model that gives them the never-ending weight gains that are the hallmark of a, "so called", good breeder. And the money and prestige this brings. After years of pursuing this program, those involved still do not understand they are trying to by-pass nature by ignoring the power of genetics. Not surprising is it?

Yes, there has been a significant increase in performance, but it was possible only when fueled with a money-gobbling ARTIFICIAL environment. Tremendous feed resources and numerous high priced inputs provide the climate for this false improvement. Mainstream breeders, not realizing or caring about the folly of their actions are nonchalantly sauntering down the road to non-sustainability.

Before going any farther we need to look back on what traits made the wild cow functional. Without proper body structure and adaptability, she would have disappeared, just as other animals did. This has to be considered when

117

setting up a successful breeding program. Ignoring these traits will lead to fighting centuries of genetic selection.

For thousands of years the only thing cattle in the wild had to do was reproduce and survive. Increased size or fast growth was not a factor. Growth was geared to what the natural environment provided. No more, no less. Any animal growing too fast or large would be out of balance with its environment and did not survive.

The traits allowing cattle to survive are fertility, skeletal structure, reasonable birthweights, along with disease and parasite resistance. Ignoring these has caused nature to push back by requiring an expensive artificial environment for survival in the modern world.

We must recognize and accept natures' limits, although this does not mean we can't work within them. We can help the cow get through a drought with some assistance as long as we don't go overboard. Our help might consist of reducing the load on resources by selling poor producers and infirm cows that would have died in the wild.

If pastures are critically mineral deficient (do not allow the mineral salesman to make this decision!), we can overcome this with just enough mineral to alleviate the deficiency. Wild cattle, not hemmed in by fences, would have roamed longer distances to get a much better mineral variety. This restriction in her environment is our doing, so an artificial adjustment is required.

By going slow, and not trying to overwhelm genetics, it may be possible to put a little faster 'natural' growth in cattle. Good pasture management may help the cow milk a little better, but not in a way that lessens her genetics when bad times roll in.

After floating my initial theory to a discussion group and taking a few pot shots, Kit Pharo, Pharo Cattle Company, posted this response.

"Nature is more concerned with survivability of the species than with anything else. We have made it possible for our cattle to survive with dystocia. We have made it possible for animals prone to parasite infection to continue to survive and reproduce. We have made it possible for hard keeping, fast growing animals to survive. We have made it possible to calve in the middle of winter. We have made it possible for the animals that used to be eliminated by drought, predators, disease, etc, etc, to survive and pass on their inferior genes to future generations. Yes, we can push past nature's limits-but nature is pushing back. Whenever we go against nature it will require more labor and/or more money. That, my friends, is how nature pushes back."

"A wealthy man is one that makes $100 a year more than his wife's sister's husband."

Unknown

SEEDSTOCK GENETICS

The seedstock industry is all about genetics, but what genetics? Genetics can be very ambiguous. Genetics can help you build a cow that survives with little care or a cow that has a great reliance on inputs for survival? Think about this? Genetics can lead you either way. Which way do you want to go? There is a world of difference in the cost of maintaining these two cows.

In an earlier piece I told about the cow that wouldn't eat cake and I assumed she would fall out of the herd. She stayed in until around age ten. I knew this had to be good genetics, which got me to thinking if, "one can, they all should." This cow had to be naturally fertile as she did it on her own.

This led me back to the seedstock people. Almost all overfeed and baby their cows. This is not natural fertility, but 'feed bucket' fertility. Without help from man, the cows would be open. Was this a type of genetics that could improve a commercial herd? NO. It would drag them down and make the cow dependent on a keeper.

Since most profitable commercial ranches are low input, buying bulls from a feed bucket herd, would be at cross-purposes. But, what do you do when almost all bulls from mainstream breeds are from that system? This management also builds in other questionable traits, which leave nothing for the cow to do by herself.

120

If bull marketing is based on high individual animal performance, you can figure cow survival traits are in jeopardy. If possible, visit the operation, especially during the winter. This will answer many questions. Calving time might also be informative. Inquire about culling strategy? Ask questions about management philosophy? Is it a standard out of the book reply? Do ranch operations and performance information appear to match philosophy?

A seedstock herd must be run in as tough, or tougher system than the commercial operation to make any improvement in the latter. This is exactly the opposite of what is occurring in mainstream seedstock herds. Ask yourself if feed bucket genetics can improve a cows' ability to survive on ranch grown forages without supplementation?

There should be no argument here, but sadly, most commercial cattlemen are still buying bulls from registered operations that are undermining their cowherds profitability. This is another example of doing the same thing over and over and expecting a different outcome.

Besides overfeeding, the cow gets copious amounts of dependent causing chemicals for parasite control. She is continually pushed for heavy weaning weights, which brings an attendant high birth weight, making her dependant on a mid-wife for calving. Overfed and babied cows don't need to travel far so feet and legs are ignored, and......well, you get the idea. It ain't good.

THE PHARO DIFFERENCE

When Kit and Deanna Pharo set out to build a herd of registered cattle, they also undertook another project. That of conceiving a philosophy that would not only be the basis for their operation, but also give direction and support to those who purchased their product. This was a drastic turn around for the norm of that era.

There was little difference among seedstock operators marketing the major breeds of the day, despite obvious variances. High animal performance was the industry keyword. Nearly everyone hewed to the same model. No philosophy attached except that of propping up cattle to make them appear productive. Place an ad in a magazine or paper touting the big numbers, attach a tagline and wait for the customers.

It was a given that big numbers were profitable. No questions asked. To get the misleading numbers being advertised required big cows, giving lots of milk, eating large amounts of grass, hay and protein. The cost of getting these numbers was never considered. With their much lower level of inputs could commercial operations come close to these figures?

This has proven to be a race to the bottom with commercial herds the big loser. It was in response to this model that Kit and Deanna began piecing together various traits that were needed in a profitable operation. This led to the fact that management had to be part of the overall solution. Genetics and management must be intertwined for success. This was an entirely new field of thought coming from a seedstock operator.

PCC would not only be selling bulls, but also defining a system that would tie their no nonsense genetics with management to make the sum of the two more profitable than each standing alone. PCC customers were told it would take more than a bull to make their operations profitable. They must also include a major change from a high input, high performance operation to one with a focus on low input, optimum production.

With the PCC newsletter leading the way, Kit gradually began to draw attention to this strategy. His no nonsense message led to speaking engagements all over the country, from large forums to small. These talks generated a flow of discussion that has become an honest appraisal of the misdirection of the cattle industry by concentrating on high performance with its expensive inputs.

From humble beginnings, with no thought of being a national influence, Pharo Cattle Company has brought attention to industry problems and a direction for continued deliberation

COMPARING VALUES

WHOSE PROFIT?

Cattlemen tend to think they are always working for THEIR profit, but is this right? In a cow-calf operation it should mean everything is done to make a cow profitable for the ranch. Sounds simple, but it can be undermined by breeding cattle geared to another segment of the industry. For years the glossies kept hammering on carcass traits, saying the end product had to be upgraded. This was to satisfy the consumer or chickens and hogs would take our market.

Big lean cattle took over when consumers said they didn't want fat on their steak. Fat was taken off genetically, even though much of this could be done in the feedlot. Why wasn't it done in the feedlot with smaller cattle? Economics. Big cattle could be fed much longer giving the feedlot increased profit from yardage fees and feed mark-up. Keeping big cattle longer is more profitable than bringing in new cattle because they don't eat as much.

Packers also wanted big cattle because cutting up the carcass of a 1500 pound critter takes very little more time than a 1100 pounder. This difference led to lower labor costs per pound of retail cut.

This may sound reasonable until you put it into perspective for the cow-calf guy hanging on at the bottom. These demands not only cut into profit, but also were not replaced by any premium from above. The upgrade service was just that. A service.

Producers that followed the advice to raise larger, fat free cattle, degraded their profit because of the increased carrying cost of the big slab sided mother that raised the big slab sided steer. Was there a premium for their calves? Probably not. Yearling folks aren't going to pay any more than necessary. If calves are held over to yearlings, is there a premium when they were sold to the feedlot? Possibly a little, but not much as it is a buyers market most of the time. No one wants to bid away THIER profit.

Taking big cattle to the feedlot is not the answer as the packer is still in control and has no desire to compensate for a big cows living cost when buying the big steer.

Where does this leave the cow calf guy who raised big cattle for the next segment? With a bloated feed bill and feed dependent cows. Does this make sense? Not in my book.

The only guy that made money, whether selling calves, yearlings or fats, was the one with small frame, easy fleshing cows with a minimal yearly cow cost. No matter which segment cattle are sold into, the biggest threat to profit is cow cost. Whatever size critter sold, it must pay the mothers expenses, be it a small thrifty cow or a big high maintenance ole' girl.

If the product price cannot be set by the producer, it is a buyers market and cutting costs is the only way the seller can survive long term. What it boils down to is concentrating on the profit most easily attained by the rancher. This will require fine-tuning management, genetics and grazing for maximum efficiency. And forgetting what the next segment wants.

There are three kinds of people;

Those that make things happen

Those that watch things happen

Those that wonder what the heck happened

Which one are you?

Try to be the first.

WEANING WEIGHT; Misconstrued
(Misconstrue; interpret erroneously)

I know you are wondering what I mean by misconstrued weight? Weaning weight is the most used and abused indicator of profitability ever devised! Yes, it is the pay weight for most producers, but does that certify its validity as an indicator of profitability? Then how did it gain such prominence as the supreme arbiter of profit?

Partly for the above reason. A very high percentage of cattlemen in this country sell calves off the cow and this weight, the heavier the better, is important to them, at least in their constricted view. Because this is their largest yearly check much weight (pun intended) is given to this sale.

Before going any further I need to explain there are two conflicting weaning weights to consider. One is the 205-day weight mainly used by seedstock producers for their breed association records and for tracking individual animal and herd progress.

The second, and most widely used, is the selling weight at the sale barn. This weight has absolutely no standards. At the coffee shop January calves out of 1500-pound cows are compared to May calves from 1000-pound cows. This is far from a fair comparison, but at the coffee shop the biggest calves, and their owner, are automatically conferred the pseudo title of, "most progressive." There will always be someone trying to lay claim to this erroneous honor, even at a bankrupting cost.

It has been said that traits easily measured become well used and acquire outsized importance just for the fact they are easily calculable. Fairbanks Morse made this one easy. It is hard to ignore, as it allows swift comparisons that have become deeply ingrained in our cattlemen culture. Once again, does it validate profitability? Nope, just 'braggin rights.'

The usual way to evaluate weaning weight is to reckon the heavier weights as more profitable. Is this certain? Not when there are ranchers NETTING more per head raising 400-pound calves than 600 pounders. Are you wondering how? It is simply the difference in level of inputs and management to raise the calf and the differential in price per pound between a heavy calf and his much-maligned lighter brethren.

Our system of pricing calves dictates how we must devise our management strategy. Both biological and economic issues must be in sync for the highest level of profit. Everyone realizes the downward trending calf price as weight goes up, but it is very hard to dislodge the thinking that extra weight is still profitable. Maybe this should be called 'gross' thinking as the emphasis is on 'gross' profit with no recognition of the cost to get there.

Is there any economic value to chasing a moving target that is going down in value as cost to do so is going up? If there were only one price per pound for calves regardless of weight, pursuing heavy weaning weights would be the best strategy. But, this is not the case so you must determine a point where the average 'unpampered' weaning weight of your calves is at the least cost. This is where net profit will be the highest.

Producers must realize that continuing to fight the downward drifting pricing system with heavier weaning weights is akin to throwing a rock to a drowning man.

A Farmer Deals with the Government Agent!

A man owned a small farm in West Texas. The wage and hour Department of Texas claimed he was not paying proper wages to his help and sent an agent to interview him. "I need a list of your employees, and how much you pay them," demanded the agent. "Well there's the my hired hand who's been with me for three years. I pay him $600 a week plus free room and board. The cook has been here 18 months, and I pay her $500 a week plus free room and board. Then there's the half – wit that works about 18 hours a day. He makes $10 a week and I buy him chewing tobacco," replied the farmer.

"That's the guy I want to talk to; the half wit," says the agent.

The farmer says, "That would be me."

Unknown

(A true story?)

DOLLARS PER HEAD COMPARISON

When coffee shop talk gets around to calf sales the common comparison is weight and price per pound. These are for bragging rights only. The real figure to look at is value per head. The reason for this is our unique system of pricing calves. The heavier they are, the less they are worth per pound.

Before scales were invented calves were priced per head. How this evolved into the present downward pricing system is not important as the focus on the present and how to understand and use correctly the information we have. Price per pound and weight of different classes are very hard to compare because as weight goes down, price is going up. To compare differing groups for profitability we must use value per head.

Value per head puts everything on the same level. With value per head, cost of raising the calves will have a direct connection to weight. From this figure net profit can be determined. This is the one that counts, but will be ignored at the coffee shop, because it takes some figuring, and just doesn't have the same gloating superiority.

Beginning in the 1970's we were confronted with all kinds of information on increasing weaning weights. From

130

universities to breed associations the emphasis on
profitability hinged on increasing weaning weights.

I began giving more thought to the profitability of
weaning weight in 1979. While at the Burlington, Colorado
sale barn I saw 500-pound calves bringing only ten dollars
a head more than 400-pound calves. Could 100 pounds be
put on profitably for ten dollars? The answer? Absolutely
not. At the time I actually was wondering if I was just too
dumb to understand how this worked. I thought I must have
been missing something. It bothered me so much I finally
got up and walked out. I drove down to a local bar to get a
much-needed drink and also to find a little resemblance to
intelligence.

As I watched the small difference in per head amounts
through the years, it became clear this was fairly common.
Occasionally the lighter calves dollared out more than
heavier calves. There are many ways to increase weaning
weights, such as earlier calving, using bulls with very high
weaning weights, cows with heavy milking ability and
increased supplementation. Many times these are all in
play. What is seldom recognized is the costs to do so can
add up faster than the value derived from these added
inputs.

The following is just one example of the many groups I
have compared through the years. I will admit that this isn't
always in favor of the lighter calves, but will be in the vast
majority of comparisons.

At the November 11, 2008 Pharo Cattle Company Fall bull sale held at Burlington livestock, Burlington, Colorado I picked up the sale sheet from their previous regular cattle sale.

I went through the sale sheet and picked out all the calves that fit in the two most common weight ranges. Here is what I found. Three batches of calves (40) weighing 432-448 and 452 pounds averaged $545.44 per head. Three groups of calves (32) weighing 547, 549 and 565 pounds averaged $573.69 per head. An advantage of only $28.25 per head for the larger calves.

The light calves averaged 445 pounds, with the heavier calves at 554 pounds. A difference of 109 pounds. What would it have cost to put on the additional weight? Let's take a look at the possibilities. The calves could have been older. The mothers might have been much larger. They may have been better milkers. Or it could have been all three. Each one of these reasons carries a direct added expense. You decide how much with your figures. What about indirect costs? If the calving was a month or more earlier in winter country the death loss and labor could be higher.

I believe it is obvious the lighter calves would derive the highest net profit when all costs are considered. When following calf sales, 400 to 450 pound calves are consistently the most profitable. This weight is easy to attain, with minimal cost. I would call this a natural weight.

Even though the above calculations will not be judged very scientific, they exist in the real world of ranching. It will vary somewhat from area to area, through the seasons and over the years, but will still be an accurate assessment when comparing weaning values. This is real world simple economics, not a page full of figures very few can understand.

When I think about the difference in value of these calves and the cost of getting the bigger calves to that state, I wonder what is the reason to do so? This has to be one of the biggest brainwashing programs ever. It is so easy to see and yet it is still going on to this day with no letting up. People are either ignoring this difference in value or claiming it just won't work for them. This is one of the easiest things to see and validate. Maybe that is the problem. We have been led to believe it must be complicated to be right. Also the American way that everything has to be bigger and faster may somehow be in the equation.

Keep a record of sale barn weights and prices from your local sale barn and do your own evaluation. Do this weekly, on a year round basis. It will be eye opening. Group them in various weight ranges, with 400 to 450 pound calves as the basis.

At the same time spend time in your office and really work on cow expenses. I have read that very few people know what their cow costs are. When you do this it must be

very truthful. Nothing can be left out. Everything must
have a realistic cost or value. If your land is owned it must
be given a value per cow. The easiest way to do this is to
charge her the local lease rate for grass. If you are putting
up your own hay, it must be valued at the going price. This
may point out the inefficiency of your operation.
Something you might not want to know.

Do you actually know what it costs you to get a calf to
selling age? Knowing this amount is absolutely critical, as
without it you are flying blind. Not knowing this is why it
is easy for the propaganda of input sellers to flim flam you
into ever-higher levels of inputs and larger weaning
weights. Read LEFT HANDED LOGIC following this for
a more informed way to figure this cost and realize what it
means.

I know of no university that runs two separate herds of
cows to do straight forward comparisons. One low input,
practical management, versus one with everything that is
recommended for profit. That is the only way for them to
be able to tell you what to do. Much of their research has
no cost/income figures. If it is available it is only for a
tightly structured program that does not take in the whole
of an operation in the real world.

I am not down on all university research, as they can do
some pinpoint work that we cannot. When we do find
research that may help us it must be charged in at a
reasonable expense for a cost/benefit comparison. I know

university people that are very knowledgeable when it comes to the real world and how it works. They may be locked into a system that does not allow them do what is best, only what the university system wants.

Cattlemen on the land must be aware of the fact that everything is going to be more expensive in the future. No expenses are going to go down long term. Only those who can turn the page and learn to cut costs and operate with the natural world as a guide will survive long-term without outside income or support.

If the above doesn't jar your thinking a little, try this way of looking at the same problem. The above calf sales example has a difference in weight of 109 pounds. If calves were sold for the same price per pound, a larger calf would be to your advantage, but how much?

For example if all calves were priced at $1.25, whether 400 or 600 pounds, the lighter calves would still be $556.25 per head. The 554-pound calves would be $692.50, amounting to $136.25 more than the light calves. The heavy calves would look better in this scenario, but would it be enough to warrant the heavier weight? It would obviously be an improvement, but still close to breakeven considering the cost of putting on the added weight.

Now take a look at what the actual value of putting on the extra 109 pounds using the figures from the original calculation above. The per head difference in value was

$28.25. Divide this by 109 pounds and the extra weight gain was worth 26 cents per pound.

Yes, that is correct! Only 26 cents per pound to put on the extra 109 pounds. How can that be profitable? It is a losing proposition any way it is judged! Not even modern math can change this outcome.

Something else to consider is that every cow will wean a certain weight calf on her own, with little supplemental assistance. This would be the cows natural ability expressed as her 'genetic equilibrium.' The definition of equilibrium is, "the state where an organism is normally oriented to its environment." Any time you try to push the cow past this equilibrium, it will involve an increased cost of some kind. If you can revamp your mind to recognize this you are on the road to even greater mind work, which leads to a more profitable operation.

"AG economists couldn't run a watermelon stand if you gave them the melons AND had state troopers flag down customers!"

Jim Hightower, former Texas Commissioner of Agriculture during the 1980's crunch.

Purdy' easy to see where he stood!

LEFT HANDED LOGIC

When figuring year-end expenses it is normal to put them on a per cow basis. This is fine, but now, it is time to figure these costs against the number of animals sold. The ones actually paying the bill. This can bring out surprising results as it puts expense recovery into a proper context.

This exercise is based on a cow calf operation. For simplicity I will remove cull cow income. This is done to concentrate on the primary income generators of the operation. Calves. More specifically, how many calves will be paying the entire cowherd cost?

To begin this example I will pull some figures out of the rafters (like some auctioneers) to build a base to figure from. We will use a 100 cow herd for ease of math. During preg checking it is found there are four open. The next spring five calves are lost in calving. One calf dies at weaning. Fifteen heifers are retained for replacements. This leaves 75 calves to sell.

These 75 calves must pay the cost of 100 cows for the year! Think about this? Instead of a per cow cost, all expenses need to be charged to the saleable animals. Looks a lot different don't it?

Let's take this a step farther. If the rancher decides to try raising weaning weights by calving earlier, and feeding more hay, he might figure an increased cost of $50 per cow. Again, is this right? No. He just added another $66.66 (50 times 100 divided by 75) for each calf to recover, before getting back to the original starting point.

Remember, every extra dollar of increased investment has to be recaptured before an additional gain can be counted. Now there is also something else to think about? The heavier calf from earlier calving is going down in price per pound, as it gets heavier. Makes it hard for this limited number of calves to generate a profit doesn't it. We just keep loading more on their backs! Doesn't make much sense when you are losing on both ends.

At this point we need to take a look at another possibility. Lets assume the rancher had a $50 hay cost per cow before the increase in the above example. He decides to revert to his granddads system and calve later to eliminate all hay feeding. This is a savings of $50 per cow, even if the cow is OPEN or has a DEAD calf! This is the left-handed logic of the title. I know this looks a little strange, but this is what happens when we CUT costs.

This is $66.66 less that the 75 calves will have to generate for a breakeven, plus because of the lighter weight, they are gaining in price per pound! This is winning on both ends.

Time To Change

The above illustrations will also work for operations holding calves over to yearlings or onto the feedlot since the offspring of any age, must support the mother.This also definitely shows the importance of getting more live calves on the ground through lighter birthweights and later calving. This will ensure spreading costs over more saleable animals, which is the ultimate goal.

The purpose of this piece is to not only explain an accurate method producers can use in evaluating management programs, but also to get the brain to thinking in a different direction. It is still okay to track cow costs per head, but to understand how they are truly affecting your operation these costs must be charged to the primary saleable animals, the ones actually carrying the load.

Every cattlemen needs to be vigilant about letting small costs creep in while concentrating on the biggest. When several of these are added up, they can amount to a substantial sum. Even little costs put more burden on the calf. These costs tend to be like paperwork lying on the desk that breed overnight. It is a never-ending battle.

Use this method anytime you are considering a management change that will incur an additional expense. This can be used to focus on problem areas, but when it is time to set benchmarks to evaluate where you are and where you want to go, another system needs to be put in place.

Just as on a grain farm, production, expenses and income should be on a per acre basis. The land base is where it all begins, so it should be the focal point of tracking progress. This will show where your management is headed. By setting benchmarks here it will help integrate cattle production with grass production. This can include only a few items or as many as you want to track.

Here are some examples. If your grazing management is improving pounds of forage production on the land, acres required to run a cow year around will be going down (you will be adding more cows) while total pounds of calf production per acre should be up (more calves total on same land base). At the same time fixed costs per cow, per acre should be going down.

Both gross income and net income per acre should be rising, but net income should be going up at a faster rate. This would show the increasing efficiency of your operation.

Sit down and use your imagination to make up a list, and then decide which will best mirror your goals and style of operation. This would also be a good time to set some goals to meet in production or cost cutting. Always keep your focus on the long term.

Ian Mitchell-Innes of South Africa related that a friend, who has a Masters Degree in Marketing, says a 1% savings

in expense is equal to a 10% increase in sales! Do you need
any more convincing? Think long and hard on this.

THE BIG DEBATE
LITTLE COW-BIG COW

This debate has been around for some time, but Kit
Pharo, of Pharo Cattle Company, with his emphasis on
cows that must live on the resources provided by the ranch,
has brought the controversy out in the open. Controversy
may be a strong word, but is applicable when listening to or
reading some of the comments non-believers make about
small cows. There are two things in play here. One is how
these smaller cows make money by fitting their
environment. Two is how the small size alone increases
income. The former will be put aside for now, as only the
small size is the subject of this piece.

Folks, it is simple economics that makes the difference,
not likes or dislikes. More small cows than fewer large
cows can be run on the same number of acres. Why the
controversy then since this is a known fact? False
assumptions are the culprit. False because true evaluations
are not used. Those who support the big cow syndrome
generally base everything on one position; that bigger is
better. That bigger makes more money by merely being

bigger. That big weaning weights are more profitable and that it takes a big critter to make money in the feedlot.

Those operating under these assumptions naturally think a big cow is the only one that makes money. It is time to look at some real world figures. Big cows eat more than little cows! Is that a big deal? Sure is. Production on the land is the deciding factor of how many animals can exist there. The following example will illustrate the difference between big and small cows. I will use 2.5% of the cows weight to arrive at relative grass consumption amounts for the two groups.

The calf weights from the Dollars Per Head Comparison will be used to determine cow sizes. Figuring a conservative 40% of cow size weaning weight, the light calves at 445 pounds might have a mother that weighs 1120 pounds. The large calves at 554 pounds, with a mother at 1375 pounds. Using the small cow as the base, at 2.5 % times 1120 pounds, gives a grass need per day of 28 pounds. Multiply this by 365 and the amount is 10,220 pounds. Using a herd number of 100 cows, the total is 1,022,000. At 2.5% the large cow consumes 34.38 pounds per day, and a yearly figure of 12,548. After dividing this amount into the yearly total for the light cows, it is evident that only 81 large cows can be grazed on the same number of acres. Since I only used steer prices in the previous example, these will be the basis for the following computations.

Since this is for comparison only it does not need to be
100% accurate. To make it a little more real life, the 75%
saleable calves from Left Handed Logic will be used. 75
light calves valued at $545.44 will dollar out at $40,908.
The heavies, 81 x 75% = 61 head, at $573.69 will total
$34,995. This gives the larger number of small calves an
advantage of $5913. Can you ignore that fact? If this
doesn't impress you think of what it will amount to over a
period of ten years. 5913 X 10 = $59,130!

This is quick and dirty, but explains the general idea of
the imbalance of the cow size quandary. Put your own
figures into the equations and decide for yourself which
way to go. There are individuals and university types who
still claim that if you live in a higher rainfall area, you can
have bigger, heavier milking cows. You sure can, but they
will not make as much money. No matter what the
environment, a greater number of smaller cows will always
return more profit. It is a simple as that.

Another point to ponder is that by spreading fixed costs
over more cows, it lowers the breakeven point of the
calves. In other words they have a higher percent of profit
than the big calves. Let's put this in round figures using
fixed land costs for better understanding. Assuming a fixed
land cost of $10,000 divided by saleable number of calves,
(75 vs 61) that is $133.33 for every small calf. For each big
calf it is $163.93. In other words the small calf is making a
profit over the land cost at $133, compared to the big calf at

$163. This $30 is another $2,250 to add to the small calf advantage.

Looks better all the time doesn't it! It is obvious the big cow folks have never applied the proper figures to a test. Or, are so mind set and arrogant they are afraid to, not wanting to be on the losing side of the argument. They would rather continue losing money than accept reality.

CATTLE RECORDS

It is often said that very few commercial operations make constructive use of their cattle records, since most are focused on performance and little else. A few people have shifted emphasis in their record keeping while many others simply quit (I fell into this category).

The P Cross Bar Ranch at Gillette, Wyoming is well ahead of the industry by applying a practical and logical use to their records. The ranch is owned and managed by Marion and Mary Scott, their daughter and husband, Marilyn and Dudley Mackey, and grandson Scott and wife Carey.

After Marion took over management of the ranch from his dad, he made several changes over the years, but not to the cattle ID and record keeping plan, except to change focus. This program, instituted by Marion's dad in the 1950's, initially concentrated on production, but is now used for culling decisions and feedlot feedback.

Finding it profitable, the ranch has been feeding their cattle many years. Thorough record keeping has aided this, through calving information, to correct problems arising at the feedlot. They have found that if there is a poor doer at the feedlot, it can be traced back to a calving problem. In one of their earlier pens, a poor doing steer was pulled and sent to the sale barn. At first poor genetics was blamed, but the following year this cow's calf performed quite well at the feedlot.

This led them back to their records to research that particular calf. They found the poor doing steer was born during a storm, became chilled, and got off to a poor start. As time went by they found that a calf that had been pulled or had scoured, would also often be a poor doer. This has prevented sending cattle to the feedlot that would not make money. Also, watching for bad dispositions has cut the number of dark cutters.

The feedlot is not the only place these poor doers show up. The records show that a stressed calf kept as a replacement heifer is usually out of the herd by age five. Using records to eliminate questionable heifers before giving them a trial can cheapen the considerable expense of developing replacements.

The Scotts' found that a search of the records after an animal was lost to bloat would show other cattle in this line had digestive problems, so all related females were culled (Culling the whole line is important. This leaves no possibility of these poor genetics cropping up again). The diligence in record keeping, evaluation and culling has made this cow herd much more efficient than the norm. The keywords are evaluation and culling, which includes recognizing a problem, a record search to find the cause, applying logic, knowledge and common sense to find an answer and then acting on it, even if it means selling several cows.

Marion states that as they quit feeding hay, and began working on cow survivability, feed conversion at the feedlot improved. The ranch has also moved calving dates from February to April and May, lessening the number of problem calves.

This illustrates the proper use of records in a commercial operation. The concentration on solving medical, environmental and genetic problems creates a direct connection to the bottom line.

Be yourself. Above all, let who you are, what you are, and what you believe, shine through every sentence you write, every piece you finish."

John Jakes

SMALL FRAME FATS

Small frame cattle became the whipping boy of the feedlot and packing industries when Simmentals, Charolais, Limousin and all the other pampered type European cattle flooded our country. Everyone was trying to get in on the surge and ride it to the top. Anyone getting in early would make mounds of money. Just breed'em big!

At about this time the battle against fat in our food was taking off. It was said that consumers wanted only lean meat and the Continental cattle were arriving just in time to save the industry.

Then Hereford and Angus joined in, making their cattle large by any means possible. Of course every breed touted their big lean cattle in the feedlot and how much money they made at the packing plant. Much of the increased income was derived from size only, which had a negative impact elsewhere.

Out on the ranch it was a different story, with calving problems the increasing and ranchers cutting back on numbers to keep these Big Mommas from running out of grass. Hay and supplement feeding increased to keep them bred and doing well. It went unrecognized that the steer in the feedlot had to pay for his mothers exorbitant living cost.

What was gained from this era of overgrown cattle? A thirty-year setback of true ranch profitability. The big cattle only helped the top end and did nothing for people on the bottom. Cattlemen were told that for the industry to survive they had to raise cattle that fit the end product. By doing this, the guy on the land was only helping the feedlot and packers gain, without doing anything for his own profit.

Net profit for the guy on the land gradually diminished as the cattle got bigger and more inputs were used. But, small frame cattle were still demonized. They were seen as getting too fat to furnish an acceptable end product. What was not being admitted was that most of the small frame problem was actually poor feeding practices. All cattle have an end point that will fit within industry standards. When they are ready, ship'em. Very few small frame cattle were fed to their advantage, giving them a black eye they didn't deserve. And it sure wasn't in the news that their cheaper living cost at home on the range would make it easier for the steer to pay his frugal mothers keep.

Enough of the way things got out of hand. It is time to learn what small frame cattle can do in the feedlot. Gary and Bobby Rhoades of Burlington, Colorado, have been entering steers in the Red Angus Gridmaster program and won the Gridmaster award twice, in 2006 and 2008.

The requirements for the Gridmaster program are:
Minimum of 30 head lot size
Minimum 85%choice or higher

Minimum 15% yield grade 4's
Minimum grid score of 100

The Grid Score balances achieving high percentages of premium products, yield grade 1's and 2's and USDA choice grade cattle with minimal percentages of yield grade 4's.

The Rhoades steers were 100% choice or higher, and only had 2.7% YG 4's. Their Grid score was 135.09. Of the 12 groups that won this award, these steers had the highest % choice, highest % premium product, and the 3rd highest overall Grid score.

As noted in another segment the P Cross Bar Ranch at Gillette, Wyoming has been successfully feeding cattle for many years. The ranch, like so many in the west was a Hereford operation, but made the change to larger cattle when production was the main focus. Several breeds were tried, but with prolapses, birthweights over 100 pounds and pulling calves from cows, the decision was made 25 years ago to switch to Red Angus. In later years the focus changed to a smaller framed cow with easier fleshing. These cows have increased survivability and the smaller frame has made little difference in the feedlot out weight of 1200 to 1250 pounds. The small frame cattle are profitable as fats and the reasonable carrying cost of the cowherd makes the lower end work also. Can't get any better than that.

RECOMMENDED CHANGES

FEED NO HAY

When changes in ranch management become the topic of conversation with the "ain't no way it will work here" folks there are three things that really bring out the denial and ridicule. The first is stringing miles of electric fence to change grazing methods, second is calving with the time selected by nature, with the third being to eliminate feeding hay.

The single largest out of pocket cost in a cattle operation is considered to be hay. Also there is a large body of data on ranch profitability that affirms the most profitable ranches are usually those with the lowest winter costs. Does this sink in with the denial bunch? Not much. The first thing they do is roll out every reason they can't quit. Feeding hay is so ingrained into the psyche that it defies all logic. And that is why it is so hard to understand what drives people to continue a practice that undercuts profitability.

How did we get into this situation anyway? Cattle have always been fed to a certain extent, but it was usually minimal, especially in ranch country. There were many reasons for heavier feeding, but the belief that the increased care of our cows would make them more profitable took hold and then the race for performance made it near mandatory.

Universities, glossy magazines and machinery sellers piled on with tons of information on what had to be done to make a profit. A cost analysis of doing all the right things was lacking, in all the hoopla. It was a given that any animal with high performance would make money. No questions asked. In some respects it could be likened to a feeding frenzy. There was little, if any, accountability.

We are now playing a new game, with new rules. With the run away cost of machinery, repairs and soon again, higher fuel prices; mechanization of ranches may regress to levels of the 1940's or 50's. The winners will be those that can hold or increase production while at the same time reducing expense. With the largest outlay of money claimed by hay, this should be the place to start. It goes hand in hand with another change, so it should make the process easier. Of course I am speaking of summer calving. Moving calving dates two or three months drastically lowers the need for winter feed. Later calving allows the cow to live off the fat on her back through winter with little assistance.

In every area of this country there are people making the change to no hay. Is it an accepted practice by their neighbors? Probably not. A few will follow, but the majority will say, "he can do it, but I can't", and then list all the reasons it won't work, but in reality, they are delineating the rut in which they are trapped.

I can't find the following quote in my jumble of papers, so the wording may not be exact, but the substance will be the same.

"Winter is less a problem of snow and cold than of the mind."
English Herdsman

STEVE & NANCY OSWALD RANCH
Cotopaxi, Colorado
Southern Colorado Rocky Mountains

The costs and values in the following are from 2005, when Steve relayed this information to me for another project.

This is a summary of costs and income Steve sent comparing his operation last year to his brothers operation in the same area. Steve calved in June and used the cows ability to use body fat stored during the summer to live off in the winter They ran on stockpiled forage with the cows doing the harvesting, stirring up the soil, fertilizing and preparing it for the next growing season.

Steve's brother calved in March, began feeding hay the end of November and quit May first, which is typical for the area. He fed about 1.5 tons per cow, at $60 a ton which amounted to $90 per cow,

They both sold steer calves the same day at LaJunta, Colorado. Steve's 390-pound calves brought $1.25 a pound for a total of $489 a head. His brother's calves weighed 562 pounds and dollared out at $523. $34 more. Did that extra $34 pay the $90 hay bill? Obviously not. When the $90 hay bill is deducted from the $523, the net is $433. $56 less than the light calves. As Steve points out, this cost savings is for hay only. It does not include labor, vehicles to feed with, maintenance, fuel, insurance, and time value of the money on the debt for the equipment, etc. Steve says it was a,, "no brainer", to move calving and quit feeding hay. If this doesn't open your eyes, what will?

This is the best example I have seen of comparing costs and income between two differing systems. It is difficult to set up parallel operations in the real world, but this is very close. The ranches are just a few miles apart, with two distinct philosophies and sold the same class of cattle on the same day at the same sale barn. I'm sure strict researchers would poke holes in this, but for us folks on the land it is real and factual.

This is important! Our system of pricing by the pound works against putting on more weight (AG version of the law of diminishing returns). When you can decrease cost, lower weights and net more money, why press for increased weight?

Now, in 2009, cattle prices have stagnated at about the same level. Are balers and swathers priced the same today as then? What about all the other expenses? The difference in value will favor the light calves even more now when increased costs are worked in.

153

Put your own figures to the above expenses, and be very truthful while doing so. Speaking from experience, I know it is very easy to under estimate expenses and over estimate income. Do not ignore the labor saved. Instead of doing something the cow should do on her own, you might have been working at something that actually made money. Feeding hay is a non-productive use of time. You can change that.

"Cows are nutrient recyclers. Balers are nutrient re-locators."
Chip Hines

An old adage should be recycled at this time.
"He who sells hay, sells his soil."

Steve Oswald, like so many others that have stopped feeding hay, now grazes his hay meadows. This recycles all the manure, urine and trods litter back into the soil, not only to retain fertility, but also raise it ever higher. The once hayed meadows are now part of the rotation. Steve said, "feeding hay was a hard habit to break, but once I did, it was surprising how well the cows did. They quit hanging around on the bottoms and stayed up on the hills where the best feed was growing." It must snow two to three feet and be very cold before he considers feeding hay and then only after a couple of days. By then it sometimes has warmed up and snow has blown off slopes, giving the cows a place to graze.

Here is another item of interest from Steve Oswald.

"One thing I should point out is that once I crunched the numbers and saw how much putting up my own hay cost me, I sold every piece of haying equipment. That cost included stuff like repairs, fuel, the labor involved, supplies like twine and tarps to cover the hay, etc., plus the opportunity cost of the money tied up in depreciating assets. It's much cheaper to purchase the little hay I now need. Haying season is one day—the day the truck shows up, instead of a month or three."

The most important fact mentioned here by Steve is the opportunity cost of the money tied up in depreciating assets. That money should be placed in an investment that is growing instead of going downhill every year. That investment doesn't have to be off ranch. It might be an improved water system, additional fencing or any thing that can contribute to increased ranch production and profitability.

Before I get to deep into this proposition, I will declare that there will be times when feeding will be necessary. During the winter of 2006-07, Eastern Colorado from the east slope on down into Kansas was hit by several bad blizzards. Feeding hay was not an option. Especially so, in this mostly short grass country. It had to be done. There will always be situations that do not fit our plans.

Warm weather on snow cover presents another problem. When snow melts on top then refreezes into ice, it is back to feeding again. Even if snow doesn't ice over, it can still reach a depth that cows can't get through. How much snow a cow can dig through somewhat depends on whether it is new fallen or fluffy snow, compared to snow that has been on the ground for a length of time and has packed down. Also, any snow that has drifted will be much harder for a cow to push her nose through. These conditions vary by area, as well as by season. This is something you and your cows will have to work out. Do not doubt your cows' ability to teach you that she is capable, if you leaver her alone. Give her a little time and then decide.

PALMER RANCH
Don & John Palmer
Boyero, Colorado

When the controversial no hay argument began stirring up folks, Don and John couldn't understand why it was such a big deal. When their granddad established their ranch in the 1930's he continued with the old way of doing things, which meant not feeding hay, except when storms were very severe. His son, Bob, followed the same practice when he began managing the ranch.

With a long-term record of successful management behind them, Don and John saw no need to change methods when they took over the ranch. Not many third generation ranchers can continue the old practices. Most want to improve on the old ways of doing things and ultimately make changes that lead to less profitability. When conditions warrant, some hay is fed. The Palmers do have a small hay shed, which is always full.

To attest to the fact that little hay is fed, Don said they took hay out one time that he was sure had been there twenty years. Amount of money saved over 75 years? Priceless! And yet their neighbors, like neighbors everywhere, ignore their success and keep on hauling hay out to their cows. Ain't human nature a funny bird to figure out?

For several years, Don and John took in cattle on pasture along with theirs. These were hay fed type cows. The first snowstorm of the season would find them at the gate waiting for a load of hay, while the Palmer cows were out rustling feed as if it was just another day.

FEEDING HAY HERE?

Until I made my first trip to Dallas, I thought feeding hay was a snow sport and I envied those who lived where it didn't snow. Then I saw hay feeding where there was no snow, but at the same time cattlemen were not feeding hay where it did snow. I'm kinda' confused?? Oh, well, I've been that way for a long time.

I live in my own little world, but it's okay. They know me here.
Unknown

157

There may be environmental differences that come into consideration. Some areas and certain grasses retain more protein and energy than others, making it easier to winter with no hay. A rancher in North Dakota says that when it gets really cold he will feed hay to keep the cows supplied with energy. He feels he has no choice, because the cows will drop condition nearly overnight.

As with everything involving cattle, many variables come into play. There are a couple of things to work on before deciding to not feed hay. Your cows must be the easy fleshing type or it will not work since they will have to live off the fat on their backs. Then move to summer calving to put the cows into a later stage of gestation during the winter. Lowering nutritional needs will make a tremendous difference in getting her through to spring. When these things are done, give it a try.

IRON DISEASE

Many men suffer from this un-researched affliction that is somewhat prevalent in the cattle raising community. This problem has been around for some time, but with the encouragement of high input ranching it really took off and has gotten out of hand. Getting hooked is easy. A certain amount of men seem to have an extra "iron" gene, which leads to a dependence on machinery.

Couple this with the desire to make labor intensive jobs easier with a machine and all is lost. It is an easy trap to fall into. It is like any other addiction (can't say no). It starts with thinking this one "simple" little machine will save hours of hand labor. Then the next step is something much bigger and more powerful. A piece of equipment that will allow greater leisure time for fishing and family.

This may sound plausible, but it just doesn't work that way. Men are married to their iron and if they aren't operating it, they are repairing it, chasing parts for it or fueling and greasing it. Saving labor? Nope. The machine begins to own them and they can't get away from its grasp. A true addiction begins in this fashion.

Iron disease is mainly a "guy" thing (spelled testosterone). This dominant gene may have been a mutation that started when the first cave man picked up a rock and made an arrowhead. Since few women have the same level of feeling about machines, I suspect they either do not acquire the gene or long ago managed to delete the DNA with their innate (def. derived from the constitution of the mind) (sorry guys) abilities.

Another possibility for the reliance on iron is that some guy's like the smell of diesel smoke. It is invigorating, giving them a sense of power. They know they are going to get something done in a hurry. Times a wasting! Is it possible there is something "addictive" in diesel smoke that keeps guy's hooked and they can't handle the withdrawal period that goes along with non-use of their big toys?

Several years ago in a conversation with a Kansas banker (plug in banker from state of your choosing) I elaborated on my thoughts of over usage of machinery and the high level of inputs in our industry. Complaining this was not only unnecessary, but also downright self-defeating. He disagreed, saying, "machinery dealers and others are a part of the community and we are all in this together." I run that thought around in my head for a couple of days and wrote the following.

THE RANCHERS VOW

From this day forward, I pledge to support my tractor, pickup, hay machinery, feed and pharmaceutical dealers through good times and bad, through drought, blizzard, flood, low prices and high interest, till bankruptcy do us part.

Funny and yet not so funny, as to a great extent, this is what we have been doing. Look at your yearly expense sheet. Does it make your knees weak? Pretty good chunk of change isn't it? Wouldn't you like to keep more of this in your pocket?

Since this is a guy problem, women are at quite a disadvantage trying to combat the situation and it is worse than they realize. Ladies, how often are your marriage vows re-affirmed? At 25 years? At 50 years? Did you know your husband re-affirms the machinery vow yearly? Did you think he was taking in the yearly equipment show to just look, touch, ogle, admire and idolize the latest behemoth? Heck no! Whenever you see a tight cluster of guy's around a salesman, rest assured, he is leading them through the 'VOW'! With a system like this you don't stand a chance.

I personally had a moderate reliance on iron for a time, but was able to kick the habit. This took time, but I knew I had to win. Three things helped me. I began a study of the natural world and realized we did not need to do all these things for the cow. Labor saving came not from machine use, but by not having a machine.

Next I found that I could work in my shop on some mechanical or welding project and get a fix without affecting my whole operation. Then I instituted a self-help counseling program when nothing else worked. Whenever I was having a severe attack of dependency I would sit down in my office and read through a big stack of fuel and repair bills. That usually did the trick. Very powerful reading, which I recommend to all who have this affliction.

THE PLUNGE

One chilly fall day Larry Renner and I went down to the
Circle Bar camp of the Collins Ranch to help Rogers and
his crew gather a pasture of pairs and ship the calves. Like
many days it started un-eventual, but didn't end that way.
And that was my fault.

As the calves were sorted off one steer was found to be
bloated. He was put into a separate pen and not shipped.
After all the trucks were loaded out, Larry, being a cattle
trader, worked out a deal to buy the bloater from Rogers.
No big deal. Yet.

We jumped the horses into the front compartment of the
trailer and put the calf in the back. When we got to Larry's
place we pulled into a large pen with several smaller pens
next to the barn. Out a way from the smaller pens was a
stock tank. I started to back up close to the smaller pen
Larry wanted to put the calf into. As there wasn't much
room to maneuver, Larry said he would just stick a rope on
the calf and we would haze him into the pen. Sounded
reasonable, I thought.

After reaching in and getting the rope on the calf, the gate
was opened. The calf at first took off in the right direction,
but that was temporary. He took off away from the little

162

pen so I grabbed the rope a few feet from his head and was trying to keep him from heading the wrong direction.

This wasn't working as he was pushing me backwards. Still not worried.

Then I felt the rim of the tank hit the back of my legs! Too late to duck under the rope! In I went, or should I say under. Larry said, "My hat floated right well." He didn't think much of my aquatic abilities though. Larry judged my backwards flip into the tank only a 1 to 1.5. Pretty low, even by non-Olympic standards. He said, "You made way too much splash on entry!"

He was quite impressed with my eruption out of the water though, saying it "Looked like a waterfall going straight up!" Needless to say as soon as the calf was in the pen I headed for home with the pickup heater on high. My horse probably wondered why I jerked the saddle off and kicked him out in such a big hurry. I headed to the house at a trot and sloshed into the kitchen where my wife Judy was working.

As I stood in the kitchen before my wife in my wet clothes and water filled boots, did I get any sympathy or even a question as to what had happened? Naw, she was laughing so hard she couldn't get enough air to talk.

FENCELINE WEANING
(ON GRASS)

Surely by now everyone has heard of weaning calves on grass across the fence from their mothers. But, how many have tried it? Not near enough I suspect. Why not? Not enough nerve? Know it "ain't" going to work? Still stuck in the high input, gotta' "baby the calf" paradigm? Enjoy all the work involved in weaning the old way?

Weaning on grass saves large amounts of labor, uses no equipment, saves the expense of the "special weaning feed" (more on this below), no feed bunks to move around, calves wean on clean and familiar ground instead of in a dirty and unfamiliar pen, wean faster and gain weight from the start. Well, do you need any more reasons than that?

There is one that I haven't mentioned and it is the biggie. Lack of STRESS! Stress makes a calf sick! Look at the stress you put a calf through in pen weaning. Away from Mom. Unfamiliar environment. Dirty environment. Possibly a disease-laden environment. Add to that the worst sort of stress. RUMEN STRESS.

Rumen stress comes with eating unfamiliar foods. Have you ever eaten something unfamiliar that didn't agree with your stomach? Think about the calf that has only had mother's milk and grass. Stuff some completely unfamiliar feed into him and what is going to happen? The microbes in his rumen are a variety that digest what he has been eating, not the strange feed.

Grain and special feeds are foreign. The rumen microbes have to begin changing and multiplying to digest the strange stuff you forced him to eat. By most reports it takes 14 to 21 days for a calf's rumen to adjust to the new feed. During the time needed to make the turn over of microbes the calf is not gaining, is under stress and this allows sickness a chance to set in.

Compare this to weaning on grass when the rumen only has to forget about milk and concentrate on grass. Actually there is little to compare. It is so lopsided only the most severely 'input challenged' (how's that for politically correct) will be able to conjure up a reason to ignore something so simple and effective.

There are a few requirements needed for success in fenceline weaning. The proper set-up will insure all goes well. First is the fence and of course it goes without saying that a good, tight fence is a necessity. Woven wire, several strands of barbed wire, multiple strands of hot wire or a combination of these will do. Think it out and use what you have available with the least amount of expense. It doesn't have to be fancy, only effective.

The area used for the calves need not be large, although it can be, as they only have to be in it for a few days and then moved elsewhere. I had a small trap that came up to my pens with a tank near the fence. The cows on the other side watered in the pen and went back out onto grass. Because of the layout, I only had to improve about 100 yards of fence. Part of it was three smooth wires with the upper and lower hot. The center wire was grounded to my steel pen fence. The rest was three barbwires with a hot wire added.

Water in the fence line or very close on the calf side is another requirement. A cow will wonder off and go to water. A calf will be walking the fence and if the water is some distance would possibly not find it. Sufficient water will help to keep them healthy and content. At least as content as removing mom can be.

With the calves in a natural environment they will begin eating grass right away. They will come to the fence regularly for the first day or so, but will continue to fill up on grass. It won't take long and they will begin grazing farther from the fence and for longer periods of time. Before you realize it they are making very few returns to the fence except for water.

Most people will separate the pairs in a pen, but it is not necessary. Marlene Moore and her husband Dwight Maseberg of the Shamrock Ranch at Wallace, NE sort pairs in the pasture. This procedure was started after taking a Bud Williams course on stockmanship. They push the cattle up to a fence not far from a gate. A few cows are sorted off, pushed through the gate, then back down a ways towards the cattle on the opposite side. Bunching the two groups across from each other keeps them comfortable.

Working easy, they continue moving cows up to the gate. The calves stay along the fence across from cows on the other side. Their mothers are there and they are comfortable on their side. Eventually all the cows are pushed through the gate. Marlene and Dwight then just shut the gate and ride to the barn.

After I got through the first year of fenceline weaning with no problems, I decided to eliminate the weaning shot I had been giving the day I weaned. I was trying to cut as many unneeded medications as possible and running them through the chute only increased their stress. It worked well as I never had a sick calf during the several years I fenceline weaned. For those who want to give vaccinations to improve sale price of calves it could be done at a later date after the calves are over the stress of weaning and it won't be nearly as hard on them.

In 2001 with the drought reaching severe levels I decided to early wean my calves. Conventional wisdom said that I had to have prepared feed and really "baby" these young calves. By that time I had quite a bit of experience with my weaning procedure and decided to ignore the smart folks. I stuck to my regular way, sorting them off and turning them back on grass. My earliest calves were born the last week in

April. On August 22, I sorted off the biggest calves, and then pulled the later calves on September 1. All calves stayed full from day one without a single sick calf. They were possibly more content and quiet than some of the older calves I had weaned. Life is good.

Weaning soaks up a lot of time, labor and expense if done in the traditional method of feeding and caring in a pen. Do you have to move bunks in and then back out later? Buy prepared feed and have it delivered or haul yourself? Make or buy hay? Feed and hay every day for ten to 20 days? Machinery to start? Fuel expense for all of the above? Buy medications and treat sick calves?

Put a dollar value on labor expended and add up all the costs. More than you thought? A yearly cost may not seem like much, but when you look at ten years savings it really adds up! Wouldn't it look good in your bank account?

Compare this to the cost of fenceline weaning. Rebuild or add a hot wire to an existing fence. Possibly make a water placement change. And these are only one times costs, which can be amortized over 20 years, or so. Costs and labor of the old system reoccur on a yearly basis!

Weight gain with fenceline weaning has shown these calves gain more the first few days, although calves weaned in other methods usually catch up later. I haven't seen any research as to the level of sickness in the various methods, but comparing notes with others that fenceline wean the consensus is that there is little or no sickness in these calves.

This is another example of needing to look at a problem from the critters view. We do unnecessary things that put stress on the cattle when we should be thinking about what is natural for them and keeping the stress off, and save money while doing it!

I'm sure some have had some difficulties with weaning in this manner. If a problem does arise a complete study of how it was implemented might show the weak spot. Possibly a few changes here and there could make it successful.

Don and John Palmer of Boyero, CO were the first in our area to fenceline wean on grass. Bob Palmer, Don and Johns Dad, was shaking his head while he was helping them set up for weaning, saying, "it wouldn't work." It worked perfectly, but Bob was still shaking his head, "wondering why they hadn't done it a long time ago."

Also from Don Palmer

"The first year we did it, a friend, Keith James was over and helped us on weaning day. Before he left he said, "I'll come back over tomorrow and help you sort them again." Now Keith is fenceline weaning and trying to convince others to do the same."

NO STRESS WEANING

Working cattle like many other things is something we have done hundreds of times and most likely haven't really considered why we do it the way we do. It was always a job that had to be done and usually the faster the better. After Bud Williams developed and began teaching his Stockmanship method of working and handling cattle, I sat back and thought about my ways. I found that I was doing some things right. Other things I knew, but didn't practice as much as I should and some things were completely new.

When we first started fenceline weaning I gave a lot of thought to what Bud said about stress. Bud is right when he says much sickness is caused by stress, and I realized we are good at piling it on cattle. Unknowingly, because few of us have ever thought much about cattle being stressed. We only worried about ourselves and the work to be done.

I began thinking about what I had been doing right and where I needed to make changes with my limited knowledge of Bud Williams technique and my own experiences. I built from there whether gathering a pasture or sorting cattle in the pen. Some things I learned were by accident. A change in weaning procedure fit into this category.

Time To Change

The second or third year of fenceline weaning I had some yearlings to the north that I wanted to take south where my cows were. I gathered and penned the yearlings and then rode out to gather the cows. When I had the cows penned I took the yearlings south to their pasture. It was about an hour by the time I got back. When I had left with the yearlings, there was a normal amount of commotion among the cows and calves bawling and looking for each other.

When I got back the pen was quiet. The pairs had all mothered up, the calves had sucked a little more and were quiet. The cows were standing quietly, or lying around chewing their cuds, seemingly, without a care. I started sorting them very easily and they almost did it themselves. At this point the proverbial light came on. They were completely comfortable. I had worked them on their terms, not mine, and they had cooperated. Later I got to thinking about how it happened.

It was about 8:00 a.m. when I had the yearlings penned and rode to the cows. They had had much of their morning fill, which was natural and made them content. Their calves had sucked and eaten a little grass. Letting them set in the pens while I shuffled the yearlings down to pasture allowed them to pair up again and the calves to suck a little more. Bellies full. Life is good.

Not only did the sorting go well, but the calves left the pens with a full belly and little stress, going to a new pasture where they began life without mom. Another plus was eating the same thing they had been eating all summer. GRASS. Life is good.

Most people have a morning routine of breakfast at a certain time, a cup of coffee or two and then getting started on their days work. How do you feel if this routine is disrupted by something unusual and hit the yard at a trot, missing your breakfast and coffee? Does this make you cranky? Hard to get along with?

Then think about that cow that has her daily routine disrupted because you want to gather at daybreak when all she wants to do is to fill her belly? She ain't gonna' like it. And how about the calf that may not have had his fill of milk? Then a drive to the pens. More chousing. Little rest. Mom and young'n can't find each other. This is stressful and makes them uncooperative. We at least have a sense of reasoning. The cow does not. She is not happy.

Spend some time contemplating your ways. It may be a surprise. You may be the one that is causing the stress and sickness that you are blaming on something else. It may actually take you longer to sort and work cattle because you are hurrying so much. Study other techniques, slow down and enjoy the work.

One person or two with the same training and thought processes can work cattle much faster and easier than a bunch of guys hollering and hurrying. As in a lot of other situations, even those not involving cattle, it is not how

FAST you go, but how SMOOTH you go. Be organized, have a plan and know what and how something is to be done. When this is done all will benefit, especially in the level of stress. You may have worked cattle hundreds of times, but did you ever think of evaluating your method in the light that it just might be wrong? Read all you can find on the subject, take a class if possible, rethink, replan, and make it SMOOTH.

The next time you wean consider gathering at a later time to allow the calves to suck and graze a little. When you have them penned, find something else to do for a while, have a cup of coffee with your wife, check your emails, staple up a mile of fence, call the banker, but do something. What, doesn't matter, as long as your pairs have time to mother up and allow the calves to suck and fill up again. The world will not come to an end if you don't jump in and start sorting as soon as the gate slams shut. Change your mind about how working cattle must be done. The stress level for both you and your cattle will come down and you will realize, life is good.

One problem with letting the cows graze and the calves suck, before gathering is the social issue. Yeah, social. What will your neighbors think if you don't ride out until 9:00 a.m. to gather? Don't you know you gotta' be cresting the hill at daylight? Lazy guy! It takes a different mindset to go against the grain. You will have to suffer some ridicule from unthinking people. That's okay though. When they are talking about you, they are giving someone else relief!

   Marlene Moore and husband Dwight Maseberg of Wallace, Nebraska work cattle as much as possible with the Bud Williams technique. The only exceptions are when neighbors are helping with the branding and shipping. Even then, with a little subterfuge, they often still manage to have their way in handling the cattle. In one instance, several riders were sent to gather 13 head from a distant pasture, while Marlene and Dwight gathered and penned several hundred pairs by themselves.

   A little girl asked her mother, "Can I go outside and play with the boys?" Her mother replied, "No, you can't play with the boys—they're too rough." The little girl thought about it for a few moments and asked, "If I can find a SMOOTH one, can I play with him?"

LET THE COW WEAN

As fenceline weaning became popular, the next step was to a more natural weaning strategy. The procedure is to leave the calves on the cows through the winter with no hay or supplement and let the cows wean the calves. This is natures' way of weaning and would have been the same for cattle in the wild. As we move to more practical ways of doing things this could be part of the plan. It also appears to be a low cost, low stress solution for the calf.

As winter progresses the cows gradually decrease milk supply and dry up, although this is variable amongst the cows. The small amount of protein the calf derives from the milk is enough for a light winter gain, which will leave them ready for a strong compensatory growth when green grass hits.

Allowing heifer calves to spend the winter with mom to learn from her will build a better cow. The teaching process becomes very important when requiring a cow to live on what the ranch produces. Every non-poisonous plant must be considered cow feed. After the mother learns what to eat, it is up to her to teach the daughter. Staying together during the winter is a critical training time as this will weed out the heifers' not adjusting to environmental conditions. Survivors of this period will vastly improve the cowherd.

Certain things need to be in place before leaving the calves on the cow. The cow must be easy fleshing to go into winter in extremely good condition, as she will be living off her fat, which is her supplement. The cows should be on a no hay program to cull those that don't have what it takes. This will pull out any lean cow that doesn't put much fat on her back, and secondly the very heavy milking cows. After two or three years of heavy culling the herd should be ready to move on.

And, last but not least, the cows must be summer calving. The cows will be in an early stage of pregnancy during winter and the calf won't be drawing much energy from the mother. This also will give the cow time to recover body condition on green grass before calving.

The cow should decrease milk production and slowly dry up and wean the calf so gradually it won't miss the milk. Some cows dry up earlier than others, or maybe even kick the calf off. This leaves them in better condition for gain back when spring comes.

I have visited with several ranchers who leave calves on until spring before pulling them off. Although everyone is a little variable as to the timing, according to their operation and weather, nine to ten months seems to be the common age to pull calves. There are several variables that can cause an early pull off. Severe weather is the most common, as harsh blizzards and unusually cold weather can put too much stress on the cow.

The cows' BCS (body condition score) has to be monitored, as she needs to go into spring with enough condition to be able to flesh up fairly fast. If she comes in too thin, she will not achieve the needed weight by calving time and this may keep her behind all summer, affecting breed back. It is normal for all animals to lose weight during the winter and then gain back when spring brings new growth.

If it is determined that the cows' are nearing a minimum BCS, it is best to pull the calves instead of supplementing her. It is said that any supplemental feed will just go to making milk instead of putting flesh on the cow, and the cow will continue losing weight.

The most difficult decision in natural weaning will be when to pull the calves if the cows are noticeably going downhill. Bobby Rhoades of Burlington, Colorado says he and his brother Gary use a minimum BCS of 3.0 to 3.5 to determine when to pull calves. They normally pull calves in April, and if the winter is mild there will be a lot of cows in the 4 to 5 range. This is a decision everyone will have to develop for their operation as there are only a few guidelines and every situation is different. The cows that should do the best are those that have been culled hard several years for survivability.

The cows in a really cold northern country will draw down much faster than in other areas, so monitoring and knowledge of the local weather environment is needed to make the decision before BCS becomes too low. At times BCS can drop rather fast when certain conditions hit.

After hearing of some ranchers having problems with sick calves and poor breed back with this system, I believe it should be approached in steps if you are unsure. Begin with leaving a portion of the calves on the cow and monitor how it works. If it seems to be suitable, try leaving heifer calves on to learn from their mothers. Then if you are comfortable and it fits into your management plan, leave them all on.

Don't fear experimenting to find what works. If you decide it isn't for you, that's fine. Ranchers don't all have to do everything the same way. As in other changes being contemplated, find out who is using this method and get first hand information. This could prevent repeating mistakes or even bring you to a decision to stick to your present plan.

"The happiest of people don't necessarily have the best of everything. They just make the best of everything that comes their way."

unknown

MAKE CALVING EASY

Winter calving is another trap in the quest for higher
weaning weights. I can't think of another logical reason for
anyone in winter country to calve at this time. At least I
think that is the reason. Or is it just tradition? Or because
dad did it and it was never questioned? In warm areas it
may be okay, but not where it gets cold and the snow
blows.

If given the choice of being born in a snow bank or on a
warm summer day, there is no doubt, which the calf would
choose. So why subject the calf to this misery? Before
going any further, I will admit I was guilty of this at one
time.

Several things become apparent when moving to summer
calving, but the one most noticed, as it is easily observed, is
the lack of stress! It is easy. It isn't even work. Anytime
you can walk out the door, in your shirtsleeves to check
cows, it has to be a huge improvement over cold, blizzards
and heavy coats.

And that is just your view. What about the calf that is
born in his summer clothes? Did you realize that? Yes, a
calf doesn't grow a winter coat until the next fall after he
goes through a photoperiod of decreasing day lengths. A
calf doesn't have the luxury of putting on a heavy coat

when the weather is bad. Calves arrive with what nature knows they should have.

A prime factor in fewer calving problems is the differing social environment between winter and summer calving. Gordon Hatfield, of Seibert, Colorado, brought this out in a discussion. His dad calved the major portion of the cows in February, with the remainder calving in August. They always had to pull several calves in the winter bunch. Gordon said that his mother watched the August cows, as they were busy farming at that time. No calf was ever pulled from the August cows.

Gordon attributed this advantage to the summer calving cows being spread out on pasture where there is little contact. The winter cows were bunched up eating hay, which allows a lot of rammin' and jammin' by cows trying to get their share of feed. A cow butting another in the last stage of pregnancy, when the calf is big, can turn the calf. The large size of the calf prevents it from straightening back around before calving. Although we tend to blame the cow, it is not her fault, but one of management. This is easily solved!

A little later the realization begins building that you are doctoring fewer calves, if any at all. A calf born in the summer has everything on his side concerning the weather. A calf can fight off sickness easier in nice weather than when it is cold, wet and nasty. Fighting the elements takes energy, which gives sickness a chance to start.

There have been reports of scours in a few herds, mine included, but nothing definite as to why. This is something that will be worked out as it is investigated. Tests to confirm what type it is may give the answer to a treatment, or more importantly, a change in management to combat the problem.

Winter calving requires hay, increased labor and fuel. For summer calving, an earlier stage of gestation during the coldest time of winter, allows a lower plane of nutrition. This becomes evident when figuring winter costs.

Producers who farm claim they can't summer calve because they don't have time to check the cows. That is a non-issue, as the cows calve themselves and rarely need your help. Using only light birthweight bulls and culling any cow that has trouble calving will enhance summer calving. I have read of people only checking cattle once a week if they have a dependable water supply.

A problem that sometimes arises is late calving cows crowding the fences of early calving cows to be near a bull as they are turned out much earlier in these herds. And those bulls enjoy jumping the fence to be neighborly. Gail Nason, of Tryon, Nebraska, says this is not much of a problem if you are using controlled grazing. With your cows on the move every few days, they are not across from other cattle for any length of time.

Another thing that helps Gail are the gomer bulls she keeps for AI heat detection. The gomers are put with the cows earlier than needed, which seems to keep the cows content and they don't go wandering and looking.

Well, with all this, what're you waiting for? After the decision is made, it is one of the easiest management changes to pull off. Just don't turn the bulls out! That's all there is to it. Just don't.

Although we never pulled many calves, the kids were usually there. It didn't dawn on me that they had seen few natural births until I overheard this conversation between my youngest daughter Dru, six at the time, and her older sister and brother. They were talking about camels when one of them wondered how they had their babies. The other replied, probably like cows. Dru piped up and said, "You mean they jack them out!"

"I'm all in favor of keeping dangerous weapons out of the hands of fools. Let's start with typewriters!"

Frank Lloyd Wright
(Uh, oh)

"Sometimes, when I look at my children, I say to myself.....Lillian, you should have remained a virgin."

Lillian Carter (mother of President Jimmy Carter)

CHANGE RECOGNIZED

It has taken many years, but a momentous change in the ranching world is gradually being accepted. New directions in grazing management are gaining in all parts of the country. A tremendous number of operations are now calving according to nature. PROFITABILITY is determining cow TYPE. A serious look at inputs is lessening their automatic dependence.

These changes are by no means being adopted by everyone in the cattle community, but it is much more popular now than 20 years ago. Kit Pharo often comments on this turning of thought in his recent presentations. In about 1993, Kit and I spoke at a seminar in Springfield, Colorado. I doubt if many knew or cared what I was talking about when I said we had to stop 'babying' our cows.

A local seedstock operator was overheard calling Kit's small framed cows, 'toads.' Well, those 'toads' are now on top and will stay there as long as success is measured by profitability. The seminar concluded with a field tour in the afternoon.

One stop was at the, afore mentioned, seedstock operators ranch. He was developing a small irrigated pasture to aid heat cycling for his AI program. This was an example of the, 'babying', I was trying to bring out. I doubt the two were put together in the minds of the attendees.

NRCS

Natural Resource Conservation Service

When I made the decision to switch from continual grazing to a controlled method I received valuable support and technical expertise from NRCS (SCS at the time) personnel. This ranged from the Steve Woodis and Carl Lovell at the local office to the Area Rangeland Management Specialist Ben Berlinger.

Carl visited my ranch to check the pipeline route, drew up specs, and took care of the paperwork. After the pipeline was installed he gave the final okay. Steve, with a wildlife degree, was interested in food plots. He encouraged me to fence off my pit for a small wildlife area. Although some bushes were planted for bird food, the primary planting was fourwing saltbush, a native plant, which had been grazed out on the hard bottoms. It is a good browse source for deer, antelope and cattle and we were interested in a possible reintroduction of the species.

Although I had read Allan Savory's book, "Holistic Resource Management", I was unsure about certain parts. Ben had been to the Savory school and helped me through much of the initial planning, which relieved a lot of stress. During occasional visits, Ben and I walked the pastures

184

checking the landscape and discussing possible changes. The thing I remember most from these walks was Ben's knowledge of plants. Not only the names, but also their value for grazing. This made me realize the great number and diversity of forbs on the prairie. I had always noticed these, but thought little about them, until learning they were a valuable resource that is usually neglected.

Julie Elliott came to Cheyenne County as a Range Conservationist my second year of grazing in the new method. Julie made general observations while looking through the paddocks, which we used in evaluations.

While writing this book I wondered why the Soil Conservation Service was so far ahead of universities and other groups in realizing Holistic Management was viable and should be adopted. I quizzed Ben about this and he filled me in on the details.

Ben and Harvey Sprock, his Northeast Colorado counterpart, were sent to the Savory school in 1983. The Colorado State Office wanted Ben and Harvey to evaluate the course and report back as to the applicability of the new and controversial way to graze rangeland. The SCS/NRCS was skeptical because this forward thinking came from an individual, not a university or another federal agency.

The story is longer than this, (and interesting) but the main point is Ben and Harvey gave the method a strong approval, which the Colorado SCS/NRCS accepted and made this their direction for range management.

UNIVERSITIES

Although I tend to get rough on universities there are many good professors and staff at most. I have met and worked with several from Colorado State University that are doing a great job and I respect their contribution to the cattle industry. I won't attempt naming them, as I would probably forget a name or two.

All universities have problems gathering up money for research, so industries with excess money at hand get in the door with their projects. In this book I continually beat the drum for those on the land that are out in front. These individuals and a few groups will be leading the way since there are no large sources of money available for a natural based, low input strategy.

Universities may do a good job with basic research, but when this is applied to practical situations it is not accompanied with a cost accounting to verify it will make money for the producer.

"I leave it up to you, my audience. If I were two faced would I be wearing this one?"

Abraham Lincoln   Lincoln-Douglas Debate 1858

SOMETHING TO THINK ABOUT

This section covers many items of differing categories. As the title suggests these are things to give some thought to that may be of interest. Or not. A few are just for fun.

DORSEY RANCH

We tend to think our methods are much better than our ancestors, but older generations used more imagination to make up for a lack of modern technology. There are several unique things about the former Dorsey Ranch northeast of Springer, New Mexico, but one of the more interesting is a 4" metal pipeline lying on top of the ground that brought water from a spring two or three miles away to the headquarters (I'm kinda' guessing on distance as it has been 45 years since I was there). The pipeline crossed several hills from source to headquarters.

After the pipeline was put in place, a vacuum was drawn on it to start the flow. The pipeline ran for years, winter and summer, until shut down for repairs. It wasn't started again before winter, which caused it to freeze and burst in many places. I don't remember when it was said the pipeline was built, but the Mansion on the ranch was begun in 1878.

If the lay of the land is correct this method could be used today, eliminating the power requirement for operating in isolated areas. Plastic pipe would prevent freeze up problems if it the water was not flowing all year. A slight problem is that the lower pressure of this system will require a larger diameter pipe than a pipeline pressured with a pump to furnish a sufficient rate of flow.

Also, the amount of fall from source to lower end will be critical for amount of water discharged. The flow could also be stopped with a valve and restarted again by opening the valve if there are no air leaks. If the prime were lost it would be easy to pull a vacuum and restart. This could also be used with a float valve or possibly multiple float valves if no air was allowed into the pipe.

This technique should also be feasible in a shallow well, if it was on a hillside so tanks could be placed lower down on the hill. Use your imagination with this and any other oldie that we may have bypassed with, "modern technology."

To save energy we may need to look at other old ways of doing things. There may be more nifty techniques out there for us modern folks to use. Maybe we aren't so smart after all. Old technology, such as using a 'free' vacuum instead of energy, to perform a job deserves to be investigated.

COW TRAILS

Did you ever wonder about something kinda' intriguing, that bothered you over the years? Something not important, but still bothering? Well, actually not even close to important, but I still wanted an answer. This little problem probably wasn't anything most people ever contemplated. Guess that says something about me doesn't it? No need to voice your opinion, I can guess. Anyway, to get on with the story, it involves cow trails. Yeah, cow trails. Now you're wondering what the heck can be intriguing about a cow trail? A path in the dirt? That's all you say?

Ever since I was a kid I wondered why a cow would wander out of a perfectly good pickup track to make her own. The track was ready made. There for the use. It didn't seem logical. But then I apparently didn't understand cow logic at the time.

The answer took about 40 years, and when it came, it wasn't an earth shaking revelation. In my head I thought it had to do with some complicated cow psychological something or other. But, no, I had to settle for something so simple that I suspect that is the reason I never thought of it.

One day, for a reason I don't remember, I was walking down a pickup track. This was several years after arthritis began taking over my ankles. It slowly sank in that my ankles were bothering me. The rounded bottom of the track put a twist in my ankles at every step.

Although not quite painful, it was very uncomfortable. What did I do? The very same thing a cow did. I got out of the trail and made my own. It was then that I finally realized what the cows did made sense. Cow trials are FLAT. The same twisting effect I experienced was bothersome to cows also!

The flat trail put no pressure on their ankles. It was then that I began rethinking many other abandoned cow trails. Any action that changed the contour of the trail made them unusable. Cows are taking care of themselves when they start a new trail. Not so dumb are they?

Now for another cow trail story. Along with cows not liking car tracks, I also wondered why cow and horse trails are narrow? When they are standing, they have a wide stance, but their trails are narrow. Now this one was probably a known fact from the first caveman to everyone since. Why was I so long on figuring this out? Dunno.

Shortly after the flat cow trail revelation, I realized what was going on with the narrow trails. Large animals, walking slowly have to place their feet under their body for balance. If they didn't they would fall over! Therefore the narrow trail. That's all. Plumb simple, but once again it took me a long time to work it out.

Are you ready for another one? I haven't come close to solving this cow trail puzzle. Why do cow trails meander so much? A cow just can't seem to keep her compass on a point. As if her ability to navigate is defective, always having to compensate with innumerable corrections. The time I have spent on this has led to almost nothing in the way of an answer.

The only thing remotely like an answer is that possibly because of cow logic, she automatically knows that water flows much more slowly down a crooked trail than a straight one. I'm ready for help on this one. If anyone has a solution, let me know.

Why so much concentration on cow trails. I'm not entirely sure, but it may have started with the many hours riding and checking cattle or riding drag behind a bunch of cows. There is a lot of time for thinking and contemplating. And that I did. When you are going along at a walk or trot, it is easy to observe what is around you. When you see something a little out of the ordinary, it stimulates the mind and starts the process of discovery. One thing I have learned through the years is that I have a 'malignant' curiosity. I may not have solved many problems, but thoroughly enjoyed the journey.

EXPECT THE UNEXPECTED

The unexpected was a clump of sand loving switchgrass down on an adobe bottom.

Ben Berlinger, Southeast Colorado Area Rangeland Management Specialist with the Natural Resources Conservation Service and I were walking paddocks when we found the switchgrass. Although in sand it is a clump grass, here it was individual plants thinly covering an area of about one foot in diameter.

This grass was definitely out of place, but why? We never determined the reason why, but in monitoring it over the years the patch grew larger in diameter to about four feet and somewhat thicker. This was nothing earth shaking, but one of the interesting things that can be found while walking and monitoring what is going on in the pasture.

IF YOU DON'T FEED HAY?

Whadya' talking about? I got to feed hay. It's a necessity. Ain't you ever heard of snow? Don't you know winter grass ain't got enough protein to get a cow through to spring? Everybody knows you gotta' feed hay. Besides, if I didn't feed hay I would be hanging around the house and my wife would put an apron on me and make me wash the dishes. Gotta' feed them cows!

Along in the mid 90's Kit Pharo invited Gary Rhoades and I to ride along with him to a gathering he was speaking to in Oklahoma. After Kit presented his program he answered questions from the audience.

One fellow was somewhat concerned about the free time he would have if he didn't feed hay. He said he would be hanging around the house, getting in his wife's way and

irritating her. Gary quickly spoke up with this retort,
"get'er a job!" Luckily (for Gary) the wife was not present.

HAY HARVESTORS

Open up any AG magazine and you will find machinery
companies extolling the virtues of their haying equipment.
Of course, all claim theirs to be the best. They are efficient
to the inth degree. They can swath and bale x number of
tons in just a few hours. After it is baled, they will even sell
you another labor saving machine to pick up and haul the
bales. Come winter they have a selection of really nifty
bale demolishers to undo what the baler did a few months
ago. Does that figure at all?

What about reliability? The swather needs regular
replacement of sickle sections. A flat tire occasionally and
numerous parts that break. Fuel has to be hauled to it and
the baler tractor. Breakdowns are regular affairs. Trips to
the dealer for parts are frustrating, especially when they are
back ordered, with no known arrival date. The machines
must have an operator on hand at all times. They have been
known to come in late or not even get there.

Now lets take a look at nature's harvester, the cow. Her
teeth last eight to ten years or so. Her runnin' gears should
last as long as her teeth. No flats. Well, maybe an
occasional foot rot. Seldom breaks down. She may expire
occasionally before the warranty is up, but not as often as a
baler. Requires no on site operator, only a part time

overseer. Is never late to work. Her fuel is the very hay that she is eating. Also she recycles everything she eats into a very useful by-product. I'd like to see a baler do that!

CANDIDATE FOR FLAT EARTH SOCIETY

Brad Young of Wausa, Nebraska was told that, "If he didn't pull at least 25% of his heifers calves, he really didn't want to be in the cattle business."

And he is still out there with many buddies. I forgot to ask Brad if he laughed or cringed at the statement?

PERCEPTION

The following is from a National Geographic article on ocean depletion and may have some insight on why ranchers are reluctant to try new grazing management techniques.

"A curious thing happens when fish stocks decline; People who aren't aware of the old levels accept the new ones as normal. Over generations, societies adjust their expectations downward to match prevailing conditions. The concept of a healthy ocean drifts from greater to lesser abundance, richer to poorer biodiversity."

Since no one is old enough in this era to have known the productivity of our grasslands 150 years ago, our only insight is from reading stories. Without direct knowledge we can only surmise from what we have read. This may affect those who can't imagine anything different than what we have now and this prevents them from envisioning possibilities of anything better.

SOIL BACTERIA

Most medically important antibiotics come from soil bacteria. Conventional wisdom holds that dirt microbes evolved these compounds as lethal weapons in the fierce battle waged beneath our feet for food and territory. For more than 15 years microbiologist Julian Davies of the University of British Columbia has been arguing otherwise. "They're talking, not fighting," Davies says.

His respected, if not wholly accepted, theory is that bacteria use most of the small molecules we call antibiotics for communication. As evidence Davies points out that in nature, soil bacteria secrete antibiotics at trace levels that do not come close to killing their microbial neighbors. "Only when we use them at unnaturally high concentrations do we find that these chemicals inhibit bacteria." he explains.

"I'm not saying that some of these compounds couldn't be used as weapons in nature," Davies says, "but that's not what we're seeing." He notes that a gram of soil contains more than one thousand different types of bacteria.

"They're all thriving there together and clearly not killing one another."
Scientific American September 2009

OPTIMUM

"To breed for optimum means to have a target in sight beyond which you don't want to go. If your goal is to maintain an optimum level for any trait, the evidence of your accomplishment is not visible change, but the lack of it,"
                    Rick Bourdon, Colorado State University

CAKE

This term can be kinda' mystifying for those not from range country or the young guys out there. Old cowboys still, 'cake their cows.' The younger generation or those east of a certain line, 'feed cubes.' How did this moniker come about? At one time cottonseed was first fed as a seed as its name implies. It was known early on as a good source of protein for cattle and other animals. The next move was to grind it into a meal to reduce bulk, for ease of handling (bagging) and also make it easier to mix with other feed.

The demand for feeding on the range brought about forcing the meal through expelling dies using pressure to press it into a block that could be fed on the ground. The expellers were of a size that allowed the product to break off in random sizes and shapes when coming out of the die.

The random sized pieces somewhat resembled pieces of a baked cake after being broken off.

When my dad worked at the Charlie Fox ranch near Wild Horse, Colorado in the early twenties, it was delivered loose in a railroad boxcar. They then scoop shoveled it into wagons to haul to the ranch and store in a shed. He said it was a guess as to how much was fed, due to the differing size pieces of cake. Although in later years round dies were used and sacking in 100 pound burlap bags became common, the term 'cake' never changed in range country.

GREG SCHWAB COMMENTS

Greg ranches near Rye, Colorado, just below the foothill of the Rockies. He made the following comments in 2003.

"Twenty years ago I calved in winter and between predators, cold weather and sick calves I went broke. Then in 1998 I read Allan Savory's book. Life in the cow deal since has been a piece of cake."

"The only vaccination I give is a 7-way at branding. I wean across the fence (three wire power fence). I have not doctored a calf in so long, I don't know if I could. I wouldn't know what to give him."

"I'm a trader. I love to buy thin late calving three year old cows' at the bottom of the cattle cycle. I've paid as little as $180. I put a good bull with them and get 1-5 calves. They're still young when the market turns around. I've sold some for as much as $850. That's real money. I do love the cattle cycle."

TRAILERS

I know most of you have pulled trailers of all kinds, thousands of miles during your lifetime, but did you ever wonder how the word 'trailer' originated? I didn't either.

I accidentally happened onto this explanation in a book. I think it may have been in the Mari Sandoz book, 'The Buffalo Hunters.' When oxen pulled wagons, a second wagon was often pulled behind the first. This wagon was called a trailer, because it 'trailed' behind the first one. Now you can wonder about something else.

GREGG MATNEY

Gregg Matney, of Lusk, Wyoming, has definite feelings about parasite and disease resistance. "We quit vaccinating and pouring our cattle several years ago. We used to Pregguard®, Scourguard®, this guard, and that guard everything. Our cattle were so GUARDED that if there was any natural resistance, it was guarded against too. There was no way to identify the cattle that didn't need it. The only way to identify these cattle is to quit everything, whether it is vaccinations, parasite control or supplementation. I was very nervous about this at first. I am now relaxing a little now because the cases of sickness have actually gone down to near zero."

THE AUSSIE VIEW

For several years a local ranch hired young guys from Australia that came over on work visas. One kid, after working on two or three ranches, and observing how things were done here commented, "In Australia we own cows, but here you are married to them and almost have to go to divorce court to get rid of them!"

A TRIBUTE TO THE HALE

Yeah, the Hale trailer. You know the one. The Oklahoma State trailer. One step above a homebuilt (some said a step below). It didn't win any blue ribbons for looks, but few ranchers cared. It was the Model T of ranch trailers. Lots of'em and they were tough, long lasting, required little care and darned sure didn't get much.

Just keep a little baling wire wrapped on the top rail and your repairs were always handy. And repairs were needed after dragging several miles down a cow path, across side hills, ditches and rocky creek bottoms.

If there weren't several feet of taillight wires draggin' it signified a road trailer or a recently repaired one (which was seldom). It was a rarity if it had more than two matching tires (when you buy used tires you take what you can get) of the same size. The original paint scheme had been blurred by streaks of green. If it didn't have at least a couple of slats broken and the top pipe swayed by a cow trying to jump out it was probably only used to haul 4-H calves to the county fair.

Hale's could and did haul about anything that could be walked in, drug in, jumped in or rolled in. The lack of a roof made it handy to roll in a 10' tank, rope it to one side and load your horse on the other. Let's see one of them aluminum monstrosities do that.

Them aluminaughts should be condemned to the interstate and not allowed on the same hallowed roads and pastures the venerable Hale rolled over. The Hale's were the workhorse of the ranch. No fancy stable breds here. The "get'er" done trailers with no frills and none needed.

Those shiny Alcoa liners just don't have any character at all. Lookin' just like so many beer cans rowed up in the ditch and about as interesting. Talk about character. Look at that Hale with the left rear corner draggin'. And that one the right corner. And there goes one with both corners rollin' rocks down the road. Doin' a pretty good job of draggin' the road. Bout' as good as most county boys can do!

200

Time To Change

Each Hale had it's own list of injuries. A slat broken here, a slat broken there, tailgate saggin', gotta' pick up on it to close, hitch bent to one side, fenders lookin' like smashed beer cans, busted taillight, a little sway backed, front sheet metal bent in by numerous jackknifes, top rail bellied in, a block of wood to dolly down on, jack wheel long since lost in some ditch crossing, and if your ole' companion Hale did suffer a near catastrophic accident, it could be repaired for about the same cost of one tire for a new fangled interstate hauler.

Every cowboy has a story about some canyon he drug a Hale into, or a coyote chase across the prairie with his Hale in tow, jumping sagebrush and only intermittently touching ground. Or the cow that he dragged in and promptly tried to jump out and high centered on the top rail. Or the guy that left his pickup in neutral while trying to drag in a bull and it rolled until the rig jackknifed or the cow that ran around the side and bent the tailgate clear to the fender.

Have you heard any wild westies about those shiny-sided trailers? Nope, but some say their trailer looks better since they wash it regularly. Wash a trailer? Hale owners would never consider such a desecration! Those varying streaks of green and brown and that pile on the fender signifies a real ranch trailer and not some highway queen.

That open topped Hale was convenient if you had a couple of cows on the fight in the trailer and you wanted to dump only one out. All you had to do was crawl up on the side, drop a loop on one, dally to the top rail and let the other one out. Try that with one of them aluminum dreadnaughts. There are only a few slits way up on the side to look in and no way-o-loopin' a critter.

Ya' gotta' get in with'em! And that can get right interestin' when there's a roof over your head and no place to save yourself.

Once the mainstay of thousands of ranches and farms, the Hale is now a discard of history along with a generation of ranchers that are also disappearing. Kinda' sad to realize we are both vanishing into the history of Ranchdom.

THE LIBRARY IS CLOSED

Recently I saw a quote that is in keeping with something that has bothered me for some time. "Every time an old person dies, a library is closed." I understand this one well. I have known several old gents that could have added to my knowledge of what the cattle industry was like before 1900.

In my teens and early twenties there were innumerable guys around that had ranched, worked on ranches or grew up in that era. I listened to their stories, but usually these occasions happened only when something came up that jarred loose a memory and the incident was recounted.

I never purposely encouraged more stories, just listened to what was being retold at the time. I don't know how many times I have kicked myself for not pursuing more information when I had a chance. These guys would have taken great pleasure in answering my questions. If only I had asked?

Ranchers and cowboys from that era wrote many books, but thousands more weren't. The words from unwritten books were lost at death. I often wonder at what I may have learned. Some things may have only been interesting, but others might have answered questions that have troubled me for years.

One thing I now understand would be what questions to ask. Fifty years ago I might have concentrated on the wrong things. And yet any knowledge would have been to my benefit. This fits the old adage, "too late smart."

I have concentrated on men, but by no means ignore women. Their experience is far reaching also. Mothers, wives and sisters were just as important in survival during tough times. The focus needs to be on the wisdom garnered in everyday living. A practical knowledge that gradually soaks in during a lifetime of confronting the rigors of life and is passed down through the years.

I gathered up a lot of information from my dad, but not nearly as much as I could have. I now can think of hundreds of things I would have quizzed him on. There were two distinct times that dad related things to me. One was while doing evening chores. It was a slower time than morning and as we were milking the cows, he nearly always had a something to talk about. It might be from the news, about his early life, or cattle. I might ask an occasional question, but usually just listened.

The other was when traveling. Dad loved to travel, especially to look at cattle. I was about twelve when he began taking me on these trips. Most were one day, but occasionally two. I look back on these times as some of my best. The conversations with the rancher we went to see were another part of my education, yet it was years later before I realized the importance. I saw a lot of country and hundreds of cattle on these trips that later became the basis for some of my thoughts. I now know I had a privileged education.

I encourage everyone, especially the younger folks, to search out the older generation and gather as much knowledge as possible. There are still many born in the 1920's that have knowledge of an earlier time, some of which would have been passed down from their ancestors. Time is running out on this priceless store of learning. Collect all you can before the library is closed. Forever.

"Tonight our worst fears have been realized. They are all gone."

Sportscaster Jim McKay covering the kidnapping and killing of the Israeli athletes by Palestinian terrorists during the 1972 Olympics.

His father once told him that, "In life, our greatest hopes and fears are seldom realized."

THE LAST WORD

My desire for this book is to convince producers to leave the high input do-it-by-our-book system. It is time to think for yourself and work out a management model with you in charge. For far too long we have been playing someone else's game. When playing a game with rules written by those selling inputs, the only one that truly wins are the rule makers.

Inputs are priced to make the manufacturer a profit, regardless of the ups and downs of the livestock market. And the middlemen follow the same structure. If the price from the manufacturer goes up, they raise prices to ensure a certain level of profit. This is where the livestock industry is trapped when cattle markets sour. There is very little reduction, if any, in input prices during the downtime of markets and drought, but just as soon as profits are glimpsed, they sure haven't forgotten how to raise prices.

Do you really believe you can win in a game like this? Will it ever change? Are you dreaming? It will get worse! As long as you are locked into their game, they will continue pitching it to you. Are they worried about your profit? Not much. All they care is if you are there to buy the product. And it you fail, there will be someone to take your place, so they aren't worried about that possibility either.

The only way to break out of the high input, no win game, is to build your management skills and become your own boss, writing the rules you want to live and operate by. Management has been replaced by inputs and this can be reversed. Management is cheap. Imagination is cheap. Just put 'em to work!

Technology was supposed to lead us to larger profits. Just allow them to show the way. They showed the way, but it was to a dependence on inputs. The more inputs used, the farther from the natural world that still has a hold on life. Disobeying the immutable laws of nature is expensive and never-ending.

Study the rules of nature and work within these parameters. Inputs will drop to a manageable level that will allow a comfortable return to your management. Nature can't be bulldozed. In some way, shape, or fashion she will have the last word. It is impossible to overcome thousands of years of genetic compounding for survival.

Emphasis should move to building soil life as new management methods reduce dependence on inputs. This is where the biggest gains will come. A finite land base leaves only one direction to go for a true increase in profits and that is in using the free inputs of sunlight, and water to enhance soils through increased understanding of plant and animal interactions.

Net profits are tied to increases in plant production, which will allow more cattle on the same land base. The operator on the land has to be in full control to chart the direction and not allow artificial inputs to replace knowledge of the natural world. This will be made easier by recognizing that input costs will always be ahead of and increasing faster than income. Don't play that game!

Do not become mired in status quo apathy. Improvements can be made in almost anything if imagination, knowledge, persistence, desire and logic are applied. Never give up or slow down the learning process, whether by studying other thought or formulating your own. A stagnating brain will give in and revert to using inputs and going to the coffee shop for support and fellowship. Find those with similar feelings, going the same direction, and a positive philosophy. The knowledge, camaraderie and support of a group like this will shorten the distance to your goals.

I know my constant referral to the natural world is beginning to wear thin, but it is the basis we must work from. Large increases in income will NEVER be derived from increasing inputs and adding a few pounds to a critter. The cost of doing this will leave very little for you. Producers are at a juncture where large income improvements are needed and these will come only by cutting costs and relying on management to replace inputs.

On many ranches it is possible to save $100 to $150 or more on cow costs by employing several of the management items discussed in this book. There is absolutely no way income can be increased by that amount.

Cattle markets occasionally make good gains, but that will be only temporary. On the other hand saving $100 will be a yearly occurrence since it has nothing to do with markets. This can be counted on. Markets cannot.

For those who haven't kept track, or are too young to know how it was in an earlier time, the gap between income and expenses has been narrowing for 45 to 50 years. To prove this I looked up some values to compare how many calves it would take to buy a pickup in 1960 compared to 2009. I did have trouble finding 1960 prices, but I think the ones used are representative for the time.

Time To Change

Steer calves weighing 450 pounds in 1960 would bring around 25 cents a pound. This is conservative as I did find some prices 2 to 3 cents more. This makes the calves worth $112.50 per head. A 1960 pickup would be in the $1600 to $1800 range. At $1800 it would require 16 calves to purchase this pickup.

I have checked several sale barns and settled on $1.15 a pound for 450 pound steer calves in September, 2009. I used an average of Ford, Chevy and Dodge plain Jane (I apologize Jane) pickups to get a value of $20,820. Folks, at that rate it takes 40 calves to buy a pickup! Over twice as many as in 1960. (I can hear the whiners saying they gotta' have more than a plain pickup. I had to use plain Jane's to give a fair comparison with the 1960 pickups. If you don't believe me go to a car show and look at the older pickups. You may not believe this, but we thought those pickups were great. If you think a $40,000 pickup is necessary over a $20,000 rig, that is a personal problem. It has little to do with making a ranch profitable).

This lesson in inflation shows the income/expense gap has narrowed significantly. And, I suspect it is worse for machinery. This is accentuated by the fact that many more inputs are purchased today than were used 50 years ago. Many of our problems are self- inflicted, which can be solved by a change in management (thinking).

Life is full of choices, from minor to major and this will never end. Now is the time to determine if a new direction is in order for continuing in business. I, and others writing on ways to survive in the cattle industry, have laid out clear-cut choices. It is now time to make a decision based on reality, not the fantasy of large increases in profit by wagering more inputs in a losing game.

Author's note

I'm sure by now you realize this is a self-published book. It has been interesting to say the least. Battling Micrsoft word and publishing templates had many frustrating moments (hours), but I feel it was worthwhile. There are some mistakes I couldn't solve so I just ignored them and worked with what I could control, which are the words I put to paper. I have many thoughts and opinions and this book is just the beginning of several, although not all will be on the cattle industry.

I encourage anyone with just a bare inclination of writing a book to get started. Join a writers group in your area if possible. The critiques, knowledge and support of these people are very valuable.

Read THE LIBRARY IS CLOSED again and think of the things you could write. Things you can share with everyone before they are lost. Books do not have to be about stupendous events. Every day happenings are interesting to those who haven't lived them. My contact information is on the last page if anyone wants to visit about self-publishing or any thing written in this book.

RESOURCES

THE STOCKMAN GRASS FARMER MAGAZINE

P. O. Box 2300 Ridgeland, MS 39157

800-748-9808

www.stockmangrassfarmer.com or sgfsample@aol.com

We send out free sample issues on request.

SGF is a monthly publication for professional graziers making a living from pasture based livestock. More profit your grassland produced in a healthy sustainable environment is what SGF is all about.

PHARO CATLE COMPANY

Cheyenne wells, Colorado

Pharo Cattle Company is a no-nonsense seedstock producer, specializing in moderate-sized, easy fleshing, forage tested bulls. Kit Pharo mails out a very opinionated bimonthly newspaper to over 20,000 producers. He also sends weekly emails to over 11,000 people. To subscribe to these publications send your request to Kit@pharocattle.com or call 1-800-311-0995. For more information go to www.pharocattle.com,

American GrazingLands Services LLC
Ranch & Grazing management consultation
Conference /Workshop presentations
Quality electric fencing & stock water products
MiG Pasture Tours
Jim & Dawn Gerrish
2222 Pahsimeroi Road
May, Idaho 83253
Tele & Fax 208-876-4067
Website: http://www.americangrazinglands.com

IAN MITCHELL-INNES

P. O. Box 52 Elandslaagte South Africa

Blanerne@mweb.co.za

Ian is a certified Holistic Instructor with an extended
knowledge of mob grazing. He makes yearly trips to the
United States teaching his popular classes

LIVESTOCK FOR LANDSCAPES

Kathy Voth

livestockforlandscapes.com

Solving pasture problems one bite at a time

Are you spending time & money because you don't know your
livestock could solve your pasture problems?

Teach your cows to eat weeds and brush

BEHAVE

The BEHAVE program focuses on research and outreach for
understanding and modifying behaviors of animals to improve
profitability, the environment and animal well being. For more
information about the BEHAVE program see our website at
www.behave.net; email: behave@cc.usu.edu or phone 435-797-
2556. You may also contact our outreach coordinator, Beth
Burritt, phone 435-797-3576 or email: beth.burritt@usu.edu

WEBSITES

DR. CHRISTINE JONES
Grazing management for healthy soils
grazingmanagement.blogspot.com

MANAGING WHOLES
Creating a future that works
www.managingwholes.com

AMAZING CARBON
www.amazingcarbon.com

Today's management is dependent on thinking more than any other time in our industry. This requires increased knowledge, but this generation has access to more information than any other in history.

The internet is a fabulous repository giving instant connection to any query. This does not lessen the need to do personal studies of nature and management, but adds increased depth to build rational solutions. There is no excuse to put research aside, since it is free and does not require you to leave the house.

A LITTLE ABOUT ME

I was born and raised on a farm and ranch southwest of Burlington, Colorado. After high school graduation in 1960, I moved to the Kit Carson, Colorado area. With ranching my goal, I worked on several local ranches, with a little stint in construction. In 1964 I met and married my wife, Judy. After working on road construction summers and helping my dad in the winter, we started on our own with leasing a neighbors place in 1968 and another in 1969.

There may never be a perfect time to start in business, but surely there are better times than just before the market dives. The 1974 cattle market crash was my first lesson in market timing and it was a good one. We barely got that one under control before the 80's came along and hit us again.

Already an amateur painter, Judy began taking art lessons along with raising our three kids and working in town during market bottoms. Judy started a sideline art business as her talent improved and in the late 1990's added sculpting along with her painting. With the addition of sculpting we decided to expand the art business and spent more time with it.

In 2002, with the drought taking hold, our son and family decided to move to Lander, Wyoming. One day I told Judy I didn't want to fight another drought and suggested we sell the cows and follow the kids to Lander. Lander had a small art community and would be a good place to further her art career. She said okay and off we went.

That was the plan, but as we all know, plans can come to a sudden halt. Two months after we moved to Lander Judy passed away. After that blow, and trying to figure out the rest of my life, I decided to take regular jobs and follow grandkids. After semi-retiring in August 2008, I moved to Yuma, Colorado to be near my son and family who also had moved back to home country.

For more information or to order books, contact
Bunkhouse Marketing

P. O. Box 469 Yuma, CO 80759

Chip Hines

970-630-6982

Hines.c.42@gmail.com